Ireland – Our Island Home
An Aerial Tour Around Ireland's Coastline

Ireland – Our Island Home
An Aerial Tour Around Ireland's Coastline

Kevin Dwyer

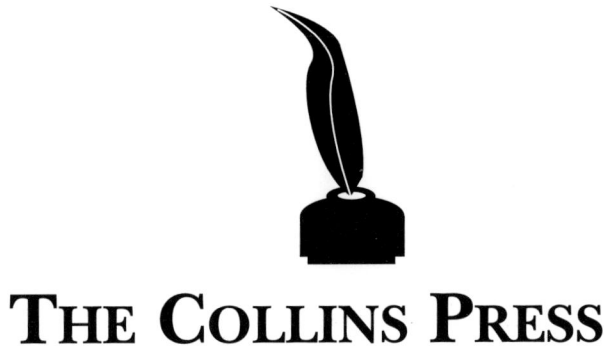

The Collins Press

Photographs
Prints and enlargements of photographs included in this book can be purchased from:
Kevin Dwyer, Photographer, Factory Hill, Glanmire, Co. Cork, Ireland.
Please write for price list.

First Published March 1997
Reprinted May 1997
Reprinted October 1997

Published by
The Collins Press,
Careys Lane,
The Huguenot Quarter,
Cork.

© Kevin Dwyer 1997

All rights reserved.

No part of this publication may be reproduced or transmitted
in any form or by any means electronic, mechanical, photocopying,
recording or otherwise without written permission of the publishers,
or else under the terms of any licence permitting limited copying issued by
The Irish Writers' Centre, 19 Parnell Square, Dublin 1.
British Library cataloguing in publication data.

Printed in Ireland by Colour Books Ltd., Dublin

Typeset by Upper Case Ltd., Cornmarket Street, Cork

ISBN: 1-898256-20-9

FOREWORD

I have slept in a swag in the north Australian Bush gazing at the Southern Cross brightly burning in an immense black sky. I have journeyed across 'The Roof of the World' in the barren mountains of Lesotho in Africa. I have sweated in rain forests, I have hacked through jungles in Thailand and Burma, I have picked cherries in Provence and cooked pasta in Verona. I have fished the Mediterranean, the Adriatic, the Indian Ocean and the South China Sea. I have seen the Northern Lights and eaten raw Reindeer and drunk Vodka in Lapland. I drove a '57 Chevrolet along route 66. I have watched alligators sliding through the mud on the Bayou and have eaten Crawfish pie and Fille Gumbo. I have landed at international airports or simple dirt strips all over the world but the only sense of real excitement and a rare feeling of contentment that I get is when my plane, on a bright sparkling day, swoops past the Sovereign Islands and the Old Head of Kinsale and squelches happily down on the tarmac at Cork Airport.

Ireland is, for me, the most beautiful country. Whether it is raining so hard that I cannot see the trees across the estuary from my garden near Kinsale, or, if like one Christmas morning we took the coast road around west Cork to Kenmare. The sky was vibrant blue like a massive stained glass window. The sea was more turquoise than the Indian Ocean and white horses danced a fandango. There was a frost, leafless fuschias and hawthorns twinkled icily in the bright morning sun. We climbed the narrowing track over the mountains which revealed a breathtaking view, more beautiful than the Pyrenees.

Through his brilliant photography, Kevin Dwyer has recorded magnificently, the contrasting beauties of this island. The spectacular shots in his book take you on a fabulous journey and it will urge you to travel over and discover for yourself the magic of Ireland.

KEITH FLOYD   Kinsale — January 1997.

INTRODUCTION

There is something about living on or coming from an island. It gives one an identity, a sense of belonging to somewhere very special. Ireland looks magnificent from the air and through this book the opportunity presents itself for me to share with others the incredible beauty of our island from above - views and perspectives that the mind just could not imagine.

Between 1992 and 1996, aerial photographic assignments have taken me around the coastline of Ireland. I have built up a unique collection of photographs which include many of the coastal towns, villages, harbours, anchorages, beaches and rivers all linked by water to make *Our Island Home*. In the book there are photographs from every coastal county on the island of Ireland, as well as some of the smaller islands off our shore. A handful of photographs have been included which were taken at ground or sea level to emphasise a particular feature or point.

The majority of photographs in the book were taken with my Hasselblad 500 ELX camera. It is my faithful workhorse and provides me with excellent results on a consistent basis. There is superb creative scope from the square composition of photographs taken with a Hasselblad.

To those magnificent men in their flying machines who have flown me in a variety of helicopters and aeroplanes for more than 9,300 miles (15,500 km) over Ireland, I have a special word of thanks. In particular, I would like to mention Batt Coleman from Kinsale who has flown and worked with me on the majority of flights for this book.

IRELAND - *Our Island Home,* will provide those of us who are Irish and those who wish they were, with a book containing a unique collection of photographs of Ireland at the close of the twentieth century and a special knowledge of a very special place.

KEVIN DWYER   Cork — January 1997.

*Through my eyes I see
Life from a different angle and
Love through my darling Fie.*

*I dedicate this book to her
and to our family
Samantha, Jayme and Julie.*

Kevin Dwyer — January 1997

We start our journey as we fly over Carlingford Lough and the north-east corner of Leinster. Heading south over the coast of County Louth, we come across the River Boyne as it flows into the Irish Sea and head along its course past the burial site at New Grange in County Meath. We head south to fly past Skerries and Malahide in County Dublin before arriving at Howth on the north side of Dublin Bay.

The weather suddenly transforms itself and we find ourselves viewing many aspects of the city of Dublin including the southern side of Dublin Bay.

We now continue south again past Greystones, Wicklow and Arklow on the relatively straight coastline of County Wicklow and take a view of *Asgard II* majestically sailing on our coastal waters. The harbours of Courtown and Rosslare bring us to the southern end of the eastern coastline. We bank and head west along the south Wexford coast, flying clockwise over Kilmore Quay and finally up the Waterford estuary past Duncarron and Ballyhack to get to the end of the Leinster Coastline.

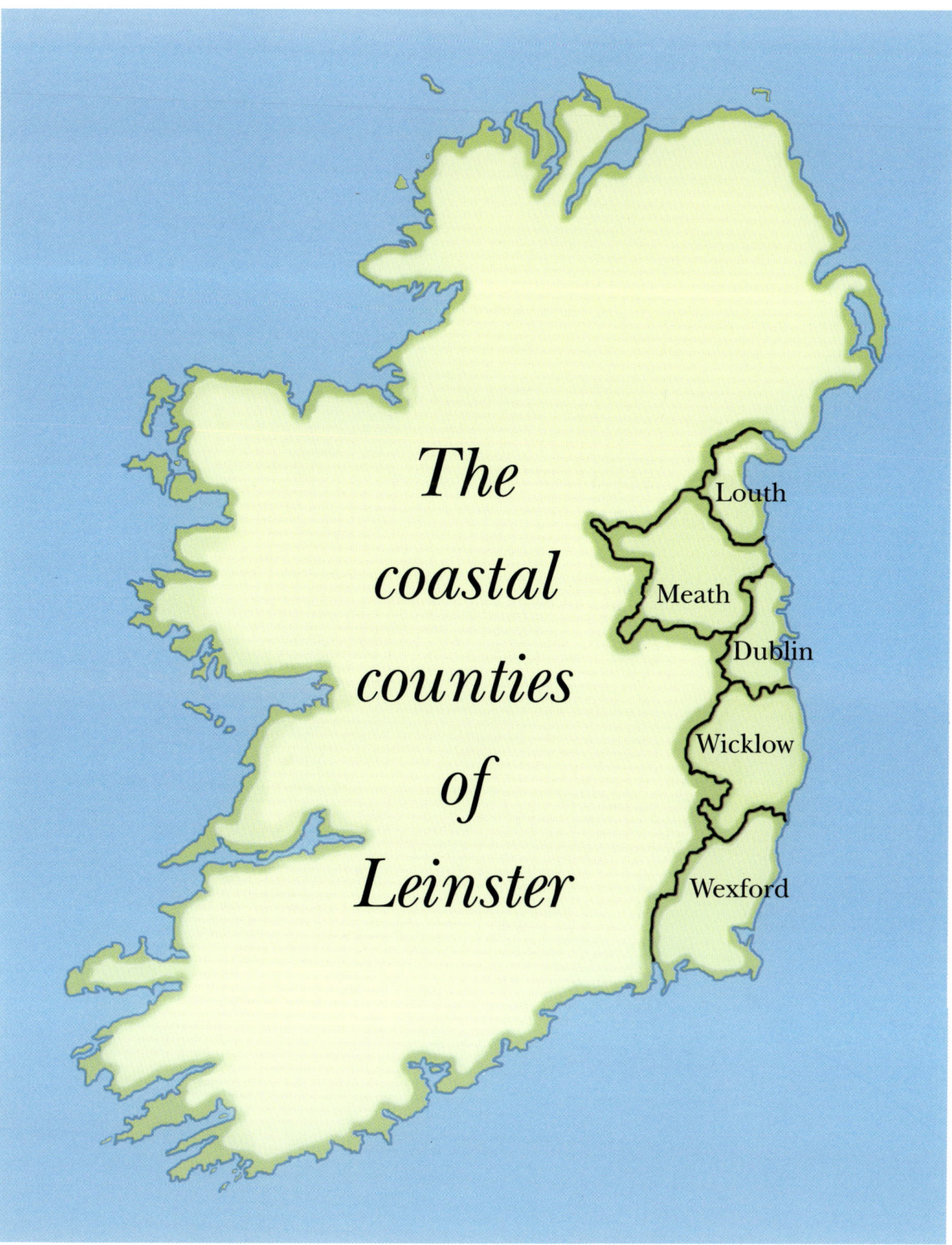

The coastal counties of Leinster

Louth
Meath
Dublin
Wicklow
Wexford

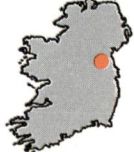 Carlingford Harbour in County Louth overlooking Carlingford Lough in the north-east corner of Leinster.

 The River Boyne entering the Irish Sea to the east of Drogheda, having flowed past the burial tomb at New Grange, County Meath, dating from circa 3000 BC.

The beach and popular town of Skerries in County Dublin and above, Malahide Inlet with the rail link from Dublin heading off to the right, north to Belfast.

The fishing and sailing port of Howth with Ireland's Eye just to the north and Lambay Island in the distance. Right, the East-Link Bridge over the River Liffey as it flows past Poolbeg and Dublin Port.

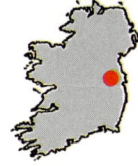 The Papal Cross and the great expanse of Phoenix Park just to the west of Dublin and above, Portobello Harbour from where, in times gone by, a three-day journey would be made on the Grand Canal to Limerick.

Merrion Square in the foreground leading to Government buildings in
Leinster House and St Stephen's Green.
Right, Dublin Castle with its circular lawn and Celtic designs.

 The campus of Trinity College Dublin with the Bank of Ireland, College Green and tree-lined O'Connell Street. Above, the harbour of Dun Laoghaire on the southern side of Dublin Bay, dotted with yachts just before the arrival of the HSS ferry from Holyhead in Wales.

Bullock Harbour with Sandycove just to the north and the James Joyce Martello Tower.
Right, Sorrento Terrace with Dalkey Island and sound,
in the distance the HSS ferry having just rounded the Kish lighthouse.

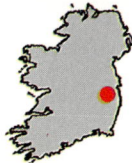
Greystones, County Wicklow. The circular end to the pier came from a base for the Kish Lighthouse. Above, the town and port of Wicklow.

Arklow, where *Asgard II* was built in Tyrell's yard in 1981, and, on the right, the sail-training vessel at the start of the Cutty Sark Tall Ships race from Cork to Belfast in 1991.

Courtown Harbour in Wexford with one of the many long sandy beaches which stretch along the shoreline of the 'Sunny South-East' and above, the ferryport of Rosslare at the south-east corner of Ireland, with direct sailings to the UK and France.

Kilmore Quay on the south coast of Wexford with St Patrick's Bridge in the distance, heading out towards the Saltee Islands and right, the fort, harbour and beach at Duncannon on the Waterford estuary.

The ferry between Ballyhack in the foreground and Passage East, linking Leinster with Munster.

Continuing our journey, we aim towards the province of Munster and start with the relatively straight coastline of County Waterford. This takes us past Dunmore East, Tramore, Dungarvan and Ardmore before climbing over the expanse of the Blackwater River and Youghal in County Cork. Similar coastline leads us to Ballycotton from where we head a little inland towards East Ferry and Cobh in Cork harbour before arriving over and around the City of Cork and Blarney Castle.

We head back to Crosshaven and the entrance to Cork Harbour, from where we fly west to the beautiful town of Kinsale, considered to be the beginning of West Cork. Big sweeping bays now greet us as we fly past Inchydoney, Glandore, Castletownshend and finally reach the southern tip of Ireland, at Baltimore. We fly around Roaring Water Bay, looking down upon Cape Clear, numerous islands, Schull and Crookhaven before eventually going out to pay our respects to the Fastnet Rock. We now fly along and explore in a fair amount of detail the fingers which stretch out from the south-west corner of Munster including Bantry Bay in County Cork and the Kenmare River, Dingle and Tralee Bays in County Kerry.

Almost mesmerised by what we have seen, we fly north-east up the Shannon Estuary to Limerick city and then back west out to Kilrush, Carrigaholt and Kilkee on the coast of County Clare. Getting close to the end of the Munster coastline, we fly north and see the magnificent sight of the Cliffs of Moher and finish this part of our journey over the village of Ballyvaughan.

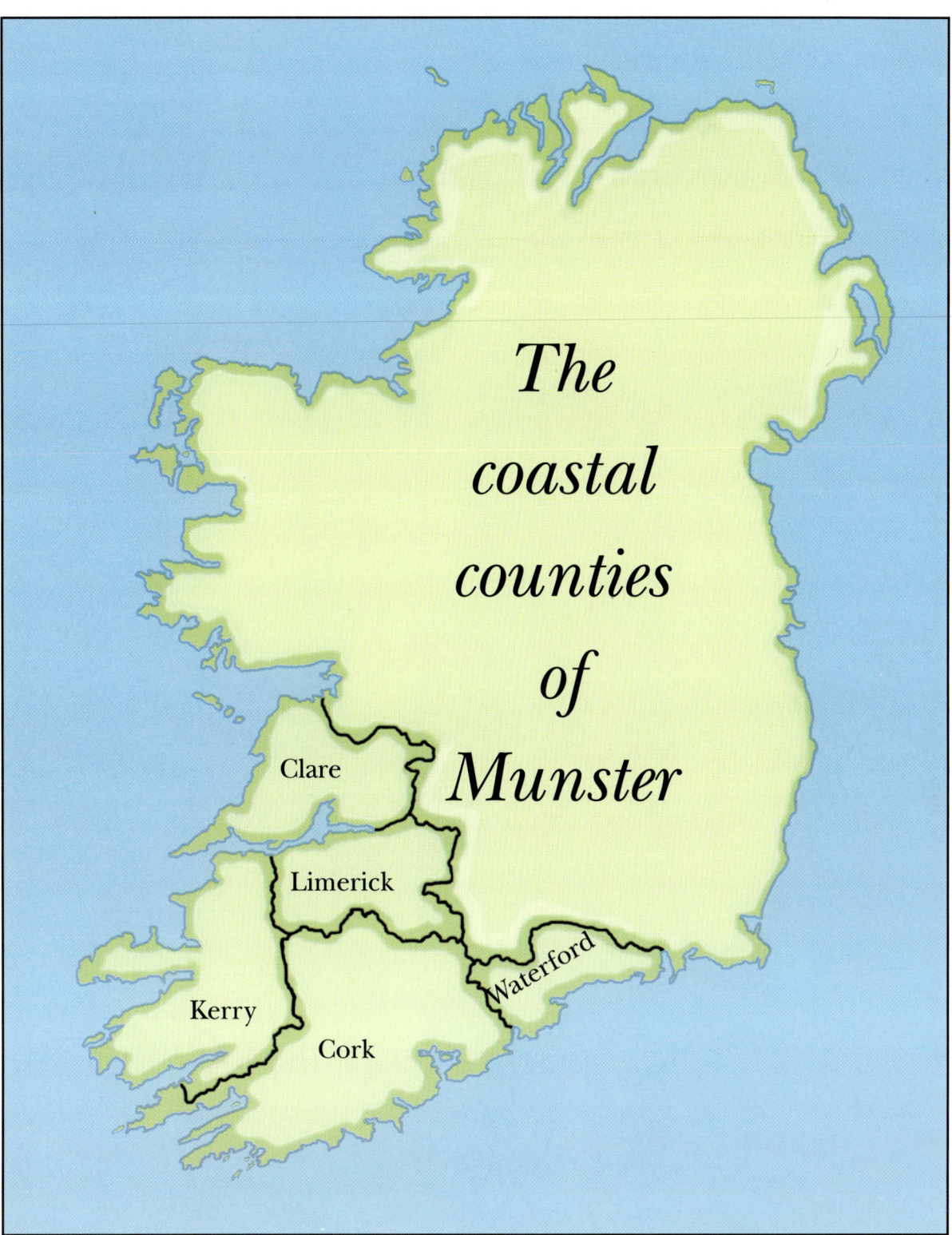

The coastal counties of Munster

The opening bridge over the River Suir and the Quayside of Waterford City.
Above, the busy fishing port and sailing harbour of Dunmore East
with Hook Head Lighthouse in the distance.

The popular holiday resort of Tramore, and, on the right, the town of Dungarvan looking across towards Helvick Head.

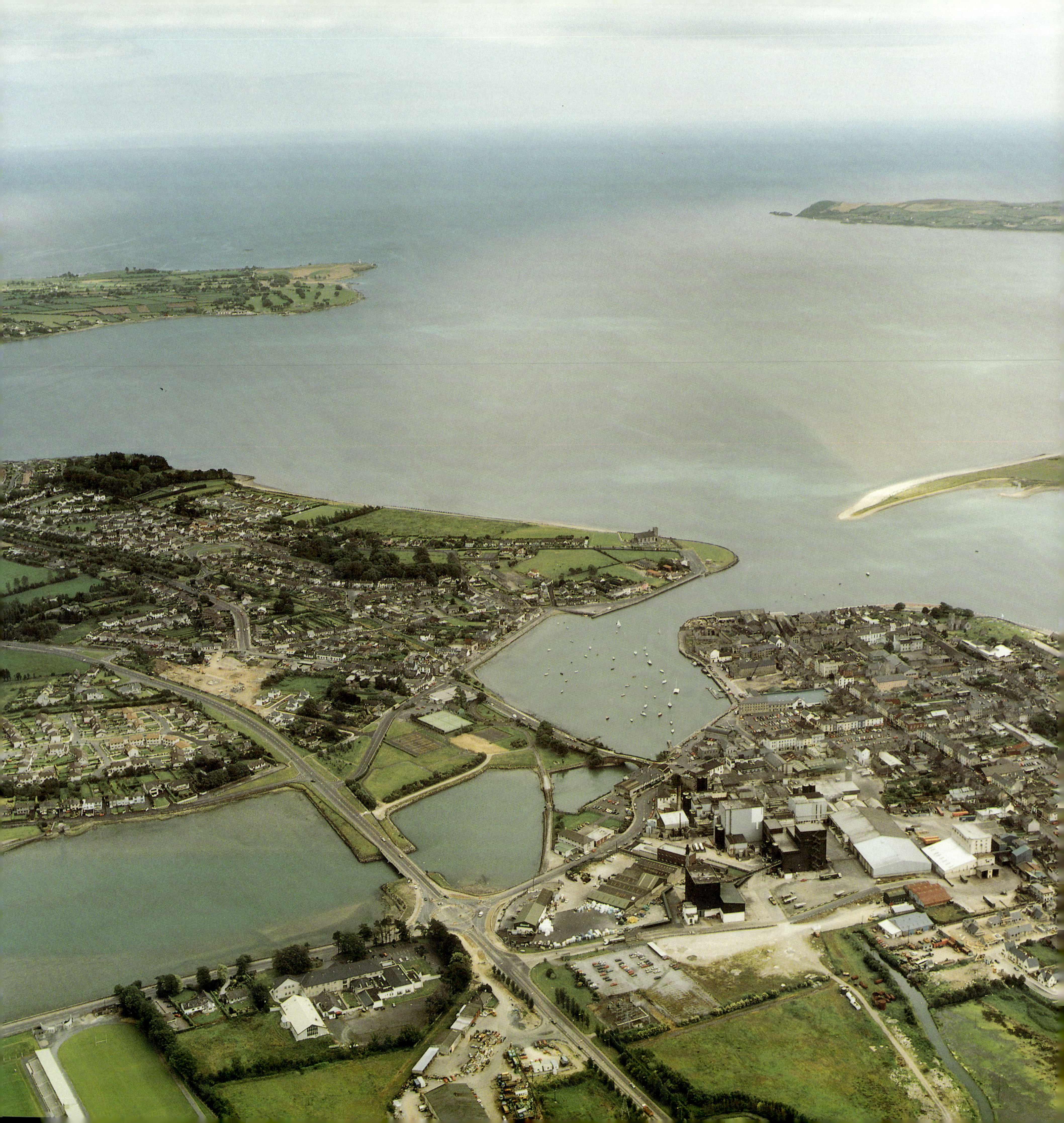

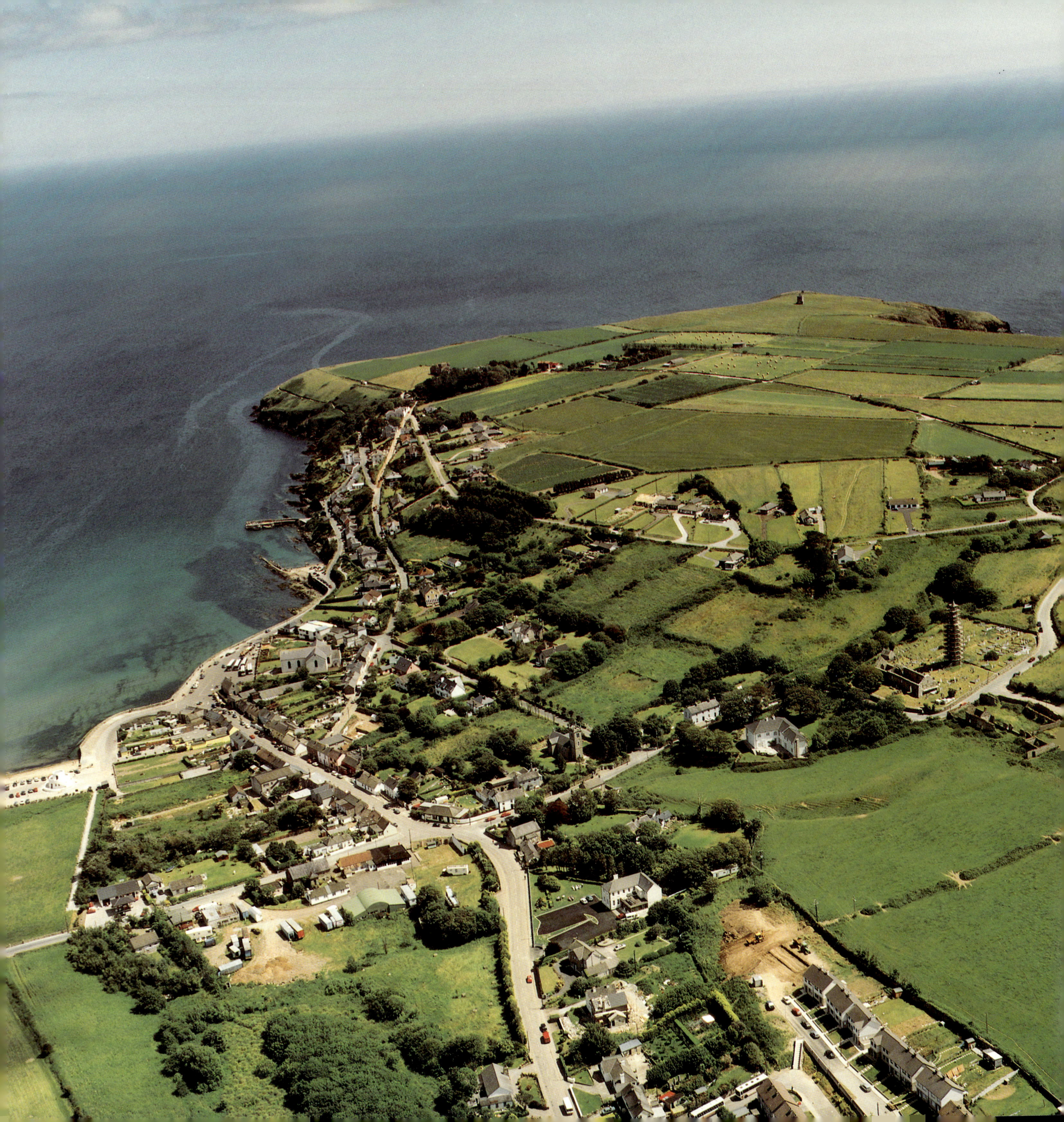

Ardmore where St Declan founded Ireland's earliest Christian settlement in 416 AD. Above, the 29m high, twelfth-century Round Tower and, inset, St Declan's Well.

The River Blackwater flowing past Youghal in County Cork. Sir Walter Raleigh cultivated the first potatoes brought back from 'The New World', when he lived here in the late sixteenth century. Right, the village of Ballycotton looking towards the harbour, islands and lighthouse.

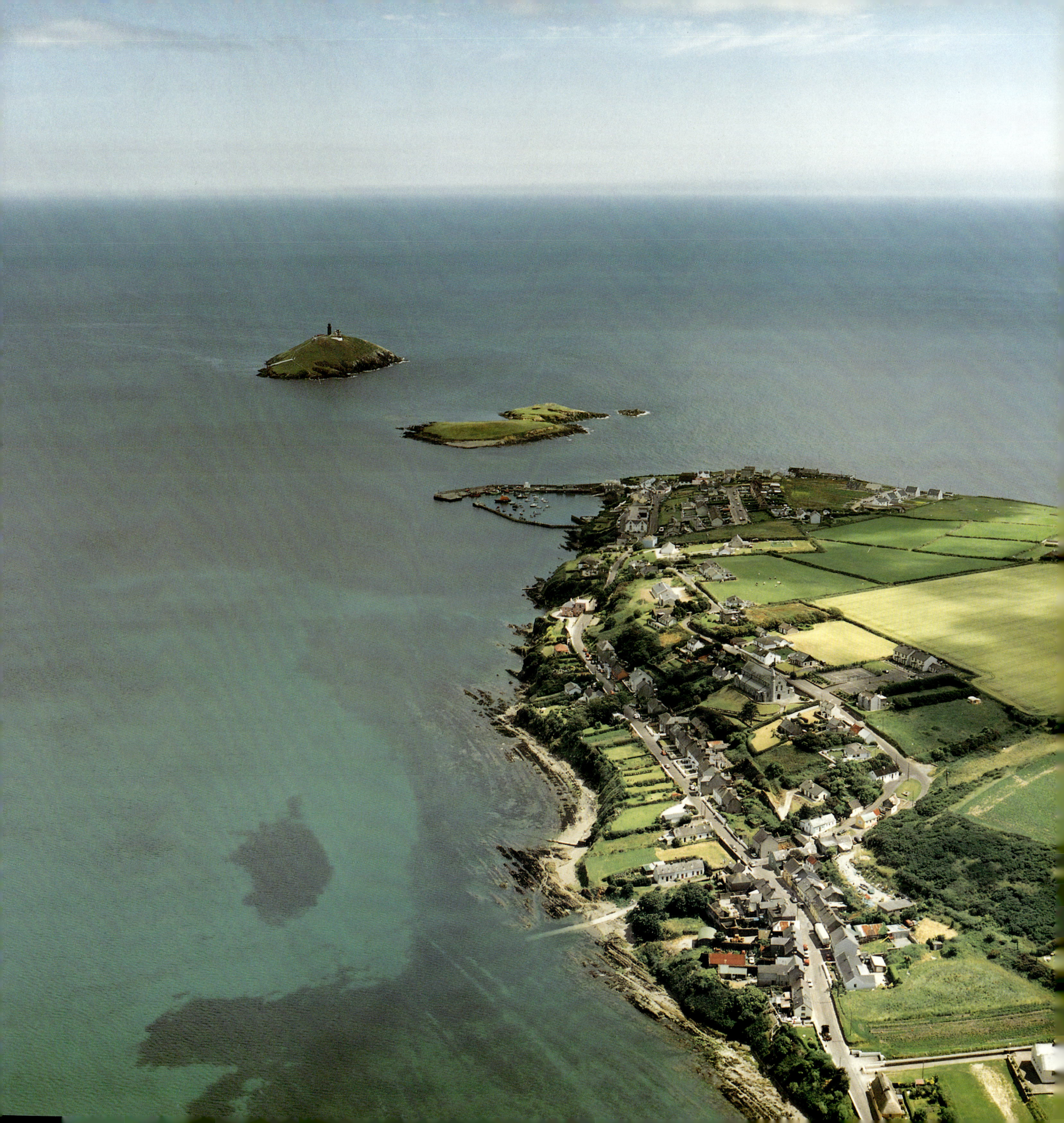

Marlogue Wood and East Ferry Marina on Great Island Cobh and right, visiting European Navies in Cork Harbour celebrating the fiftieth anniversary of the Irish Naval Service in June 1996. Inset, the stately town of Cobh.

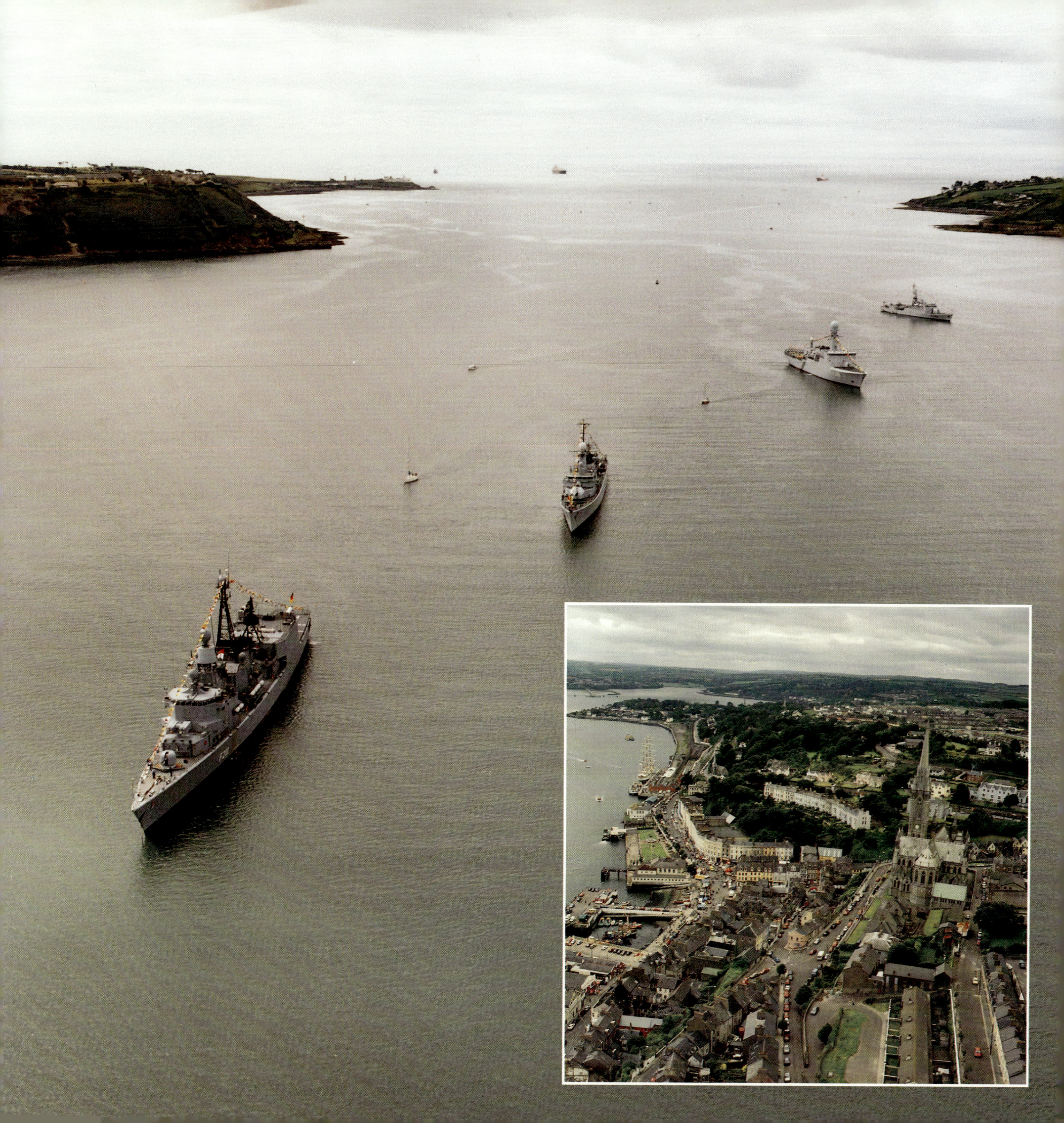

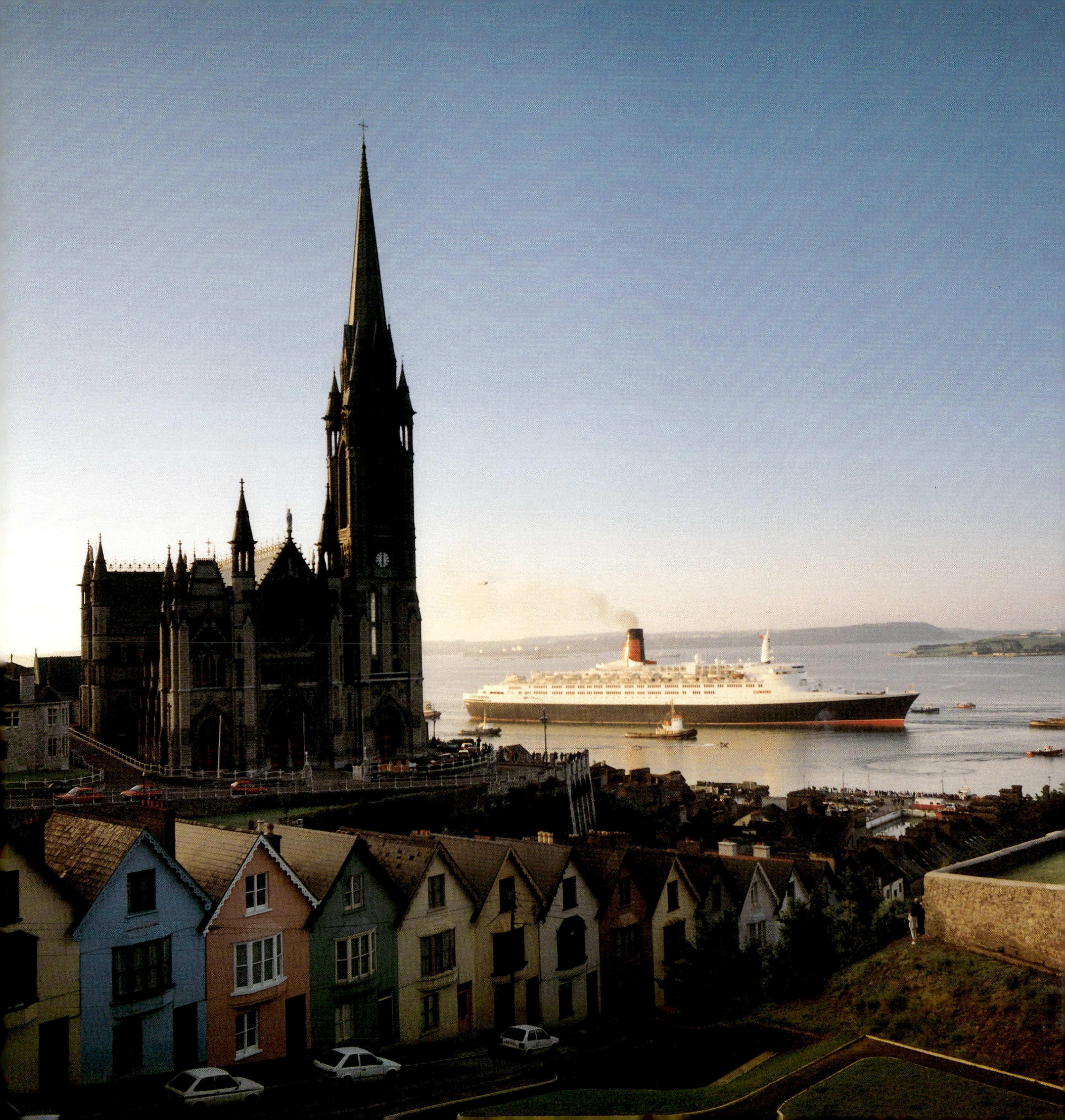

The great era of liners regularly visiting the Port of Cork brought back to life by a visit of the QE2 as she passes St Colman's Cathedral, Cobh, and above, the small village of Glounthaune on an estuary within Cork harbour.

Looking westwards over Cork City with its many bridges and the divide in the River Lee and right, the heart of old Cork with St Ann's Shandon overlooking the River Lee as it weaves past the Mardyke.

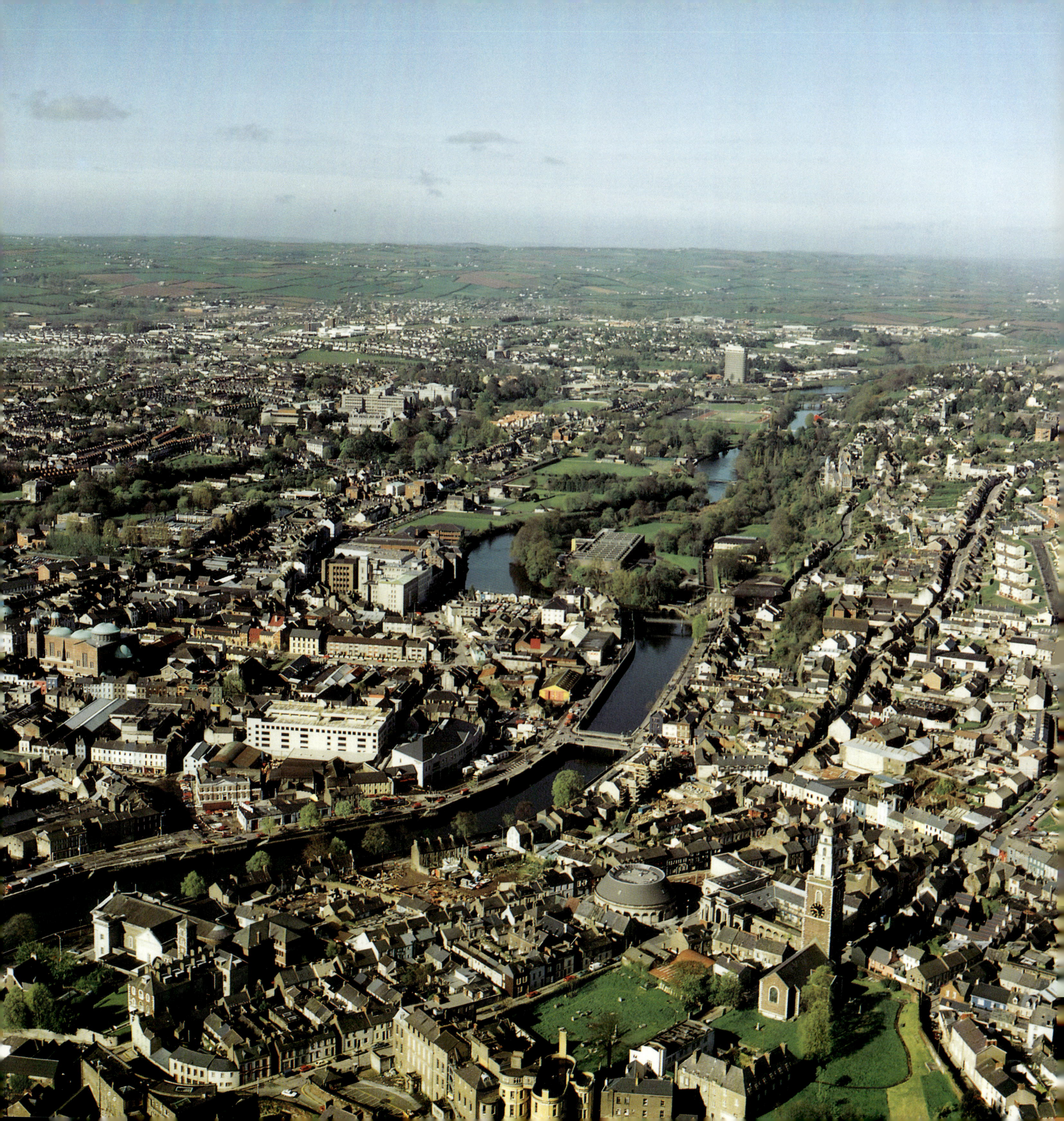

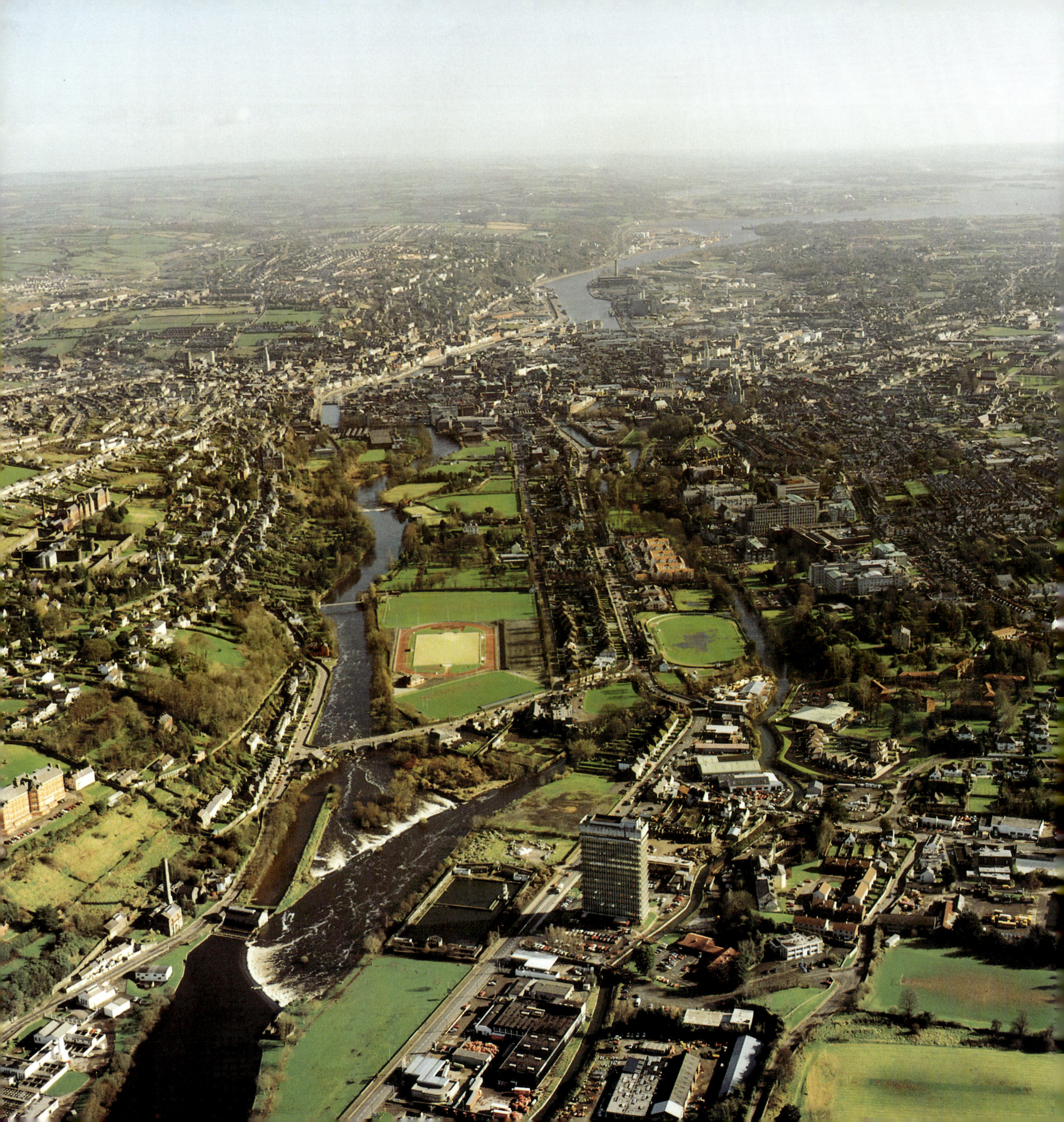

Looking east over the County Hall, University College Cork and the City.
Above, visitors on the ramparts of Blarney Castle to kiss the stone
and acquire eloquence through 'The Gift of the Gab'.

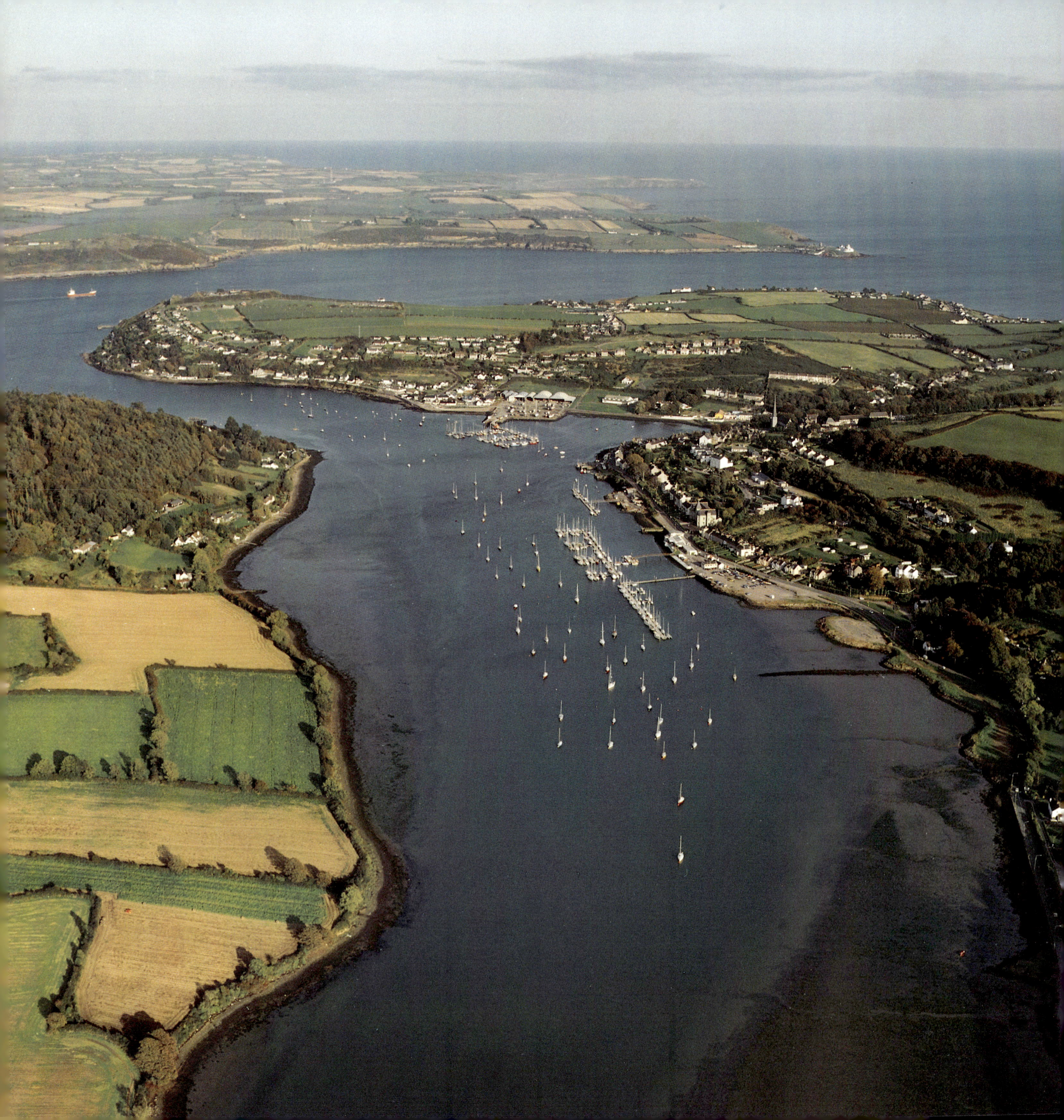

Crosshaven on the Owenabue River and Roches Point at the entrance to Cork Harbour and above, Kinsale – Ireland's oldest town.

Kinsale from the south-east and right the marina with yachts from the Cruising Club of America, Clyde Cruising Club, New York Yacht Club and Royal Cruising Club assembling in July 1996 for the Irish Cruising Club 'Cruise in Company' along the south coast.

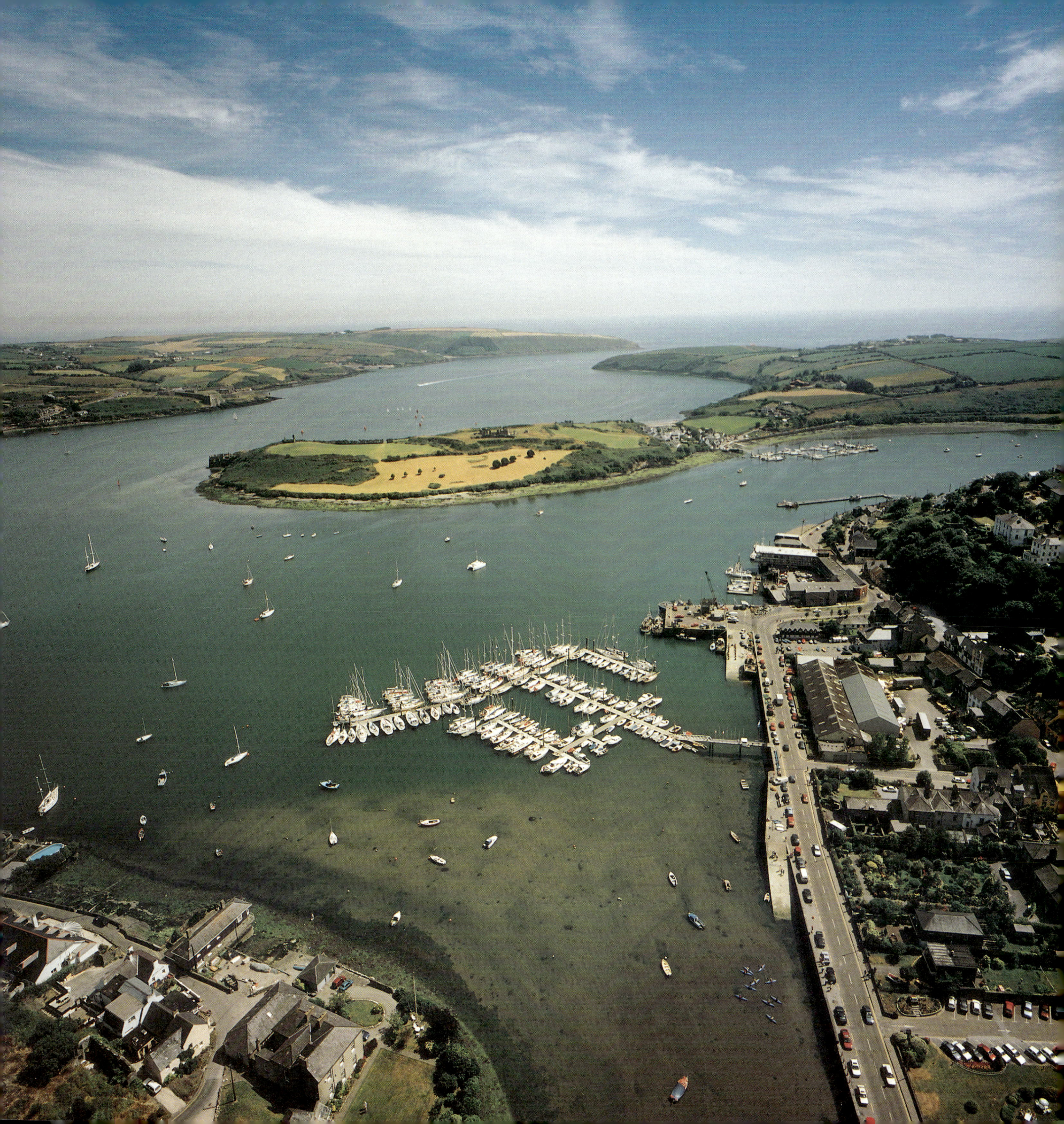

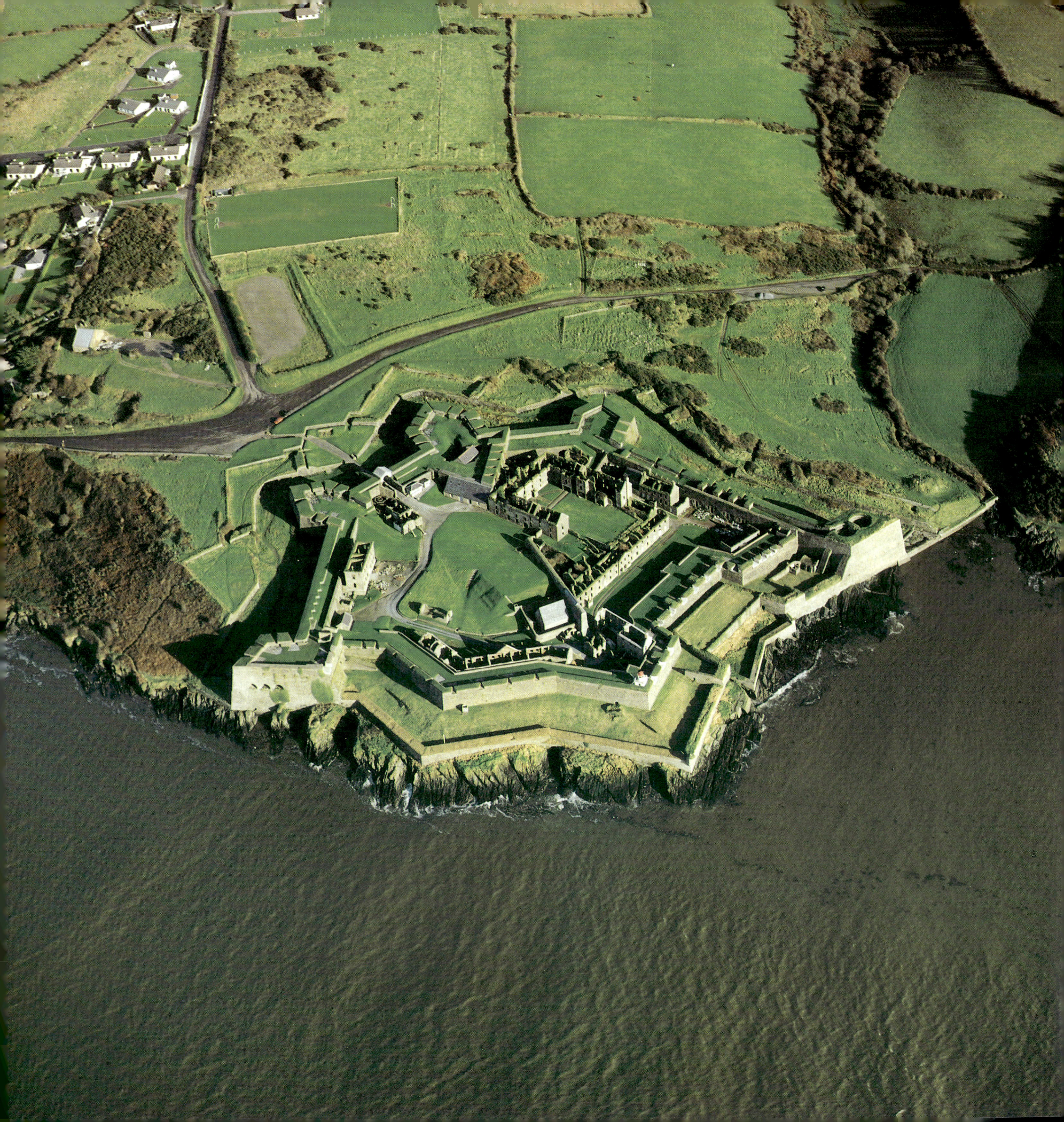

Charles Fort, Kinsale, with long winter shadows on a December morning
and above, the beach at Inchydoney near Clonakilty in west Cork.

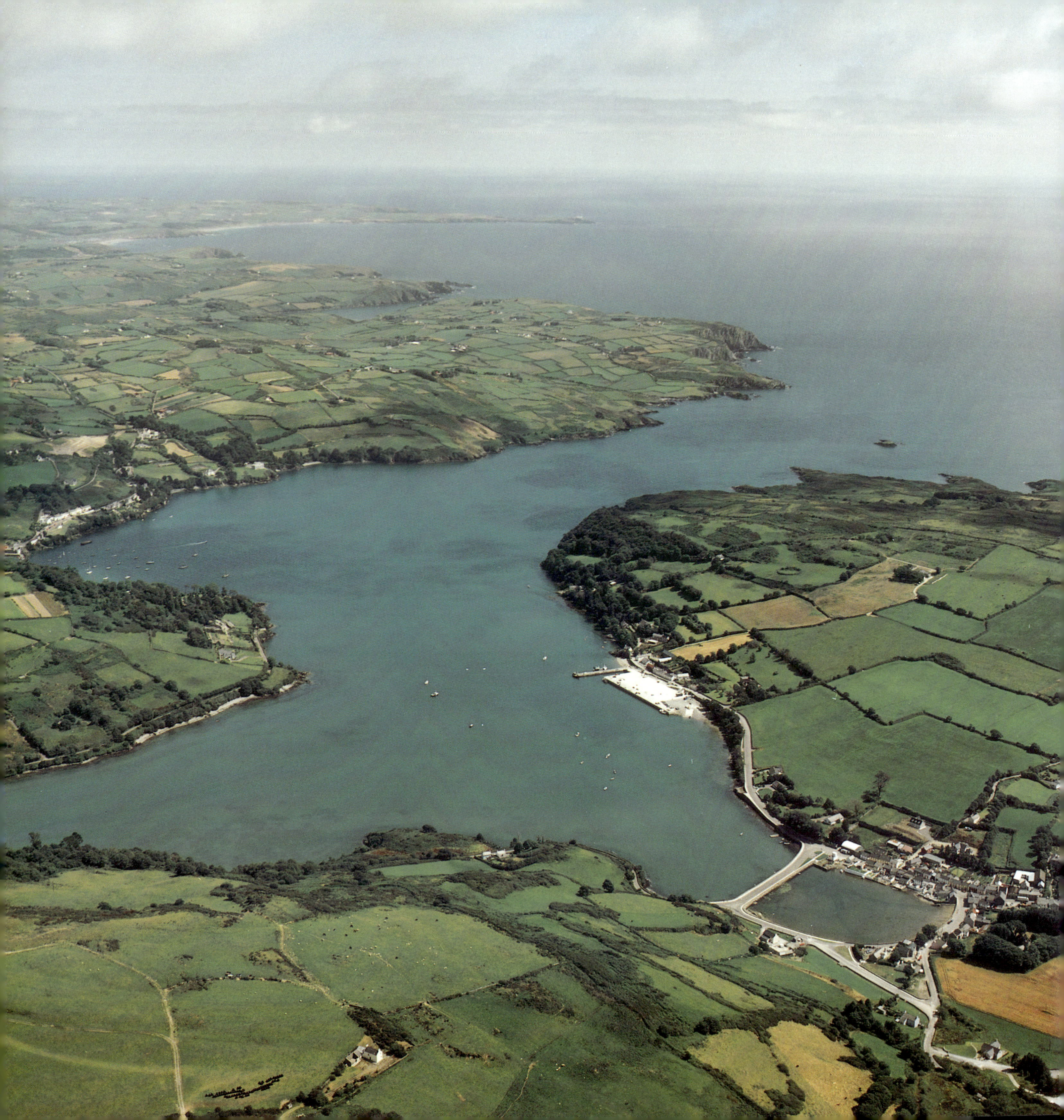

The villages of Glandore on the left of the photograph and Union Hall
with its new fisheries pier to the right.
Above, the steep hill in the village of Castletownshend, flattened through aerial perspective.

Baltimore Harbour, the southern tip of the Island of Ireland and two views of North Harbour on Cape Clear Island.

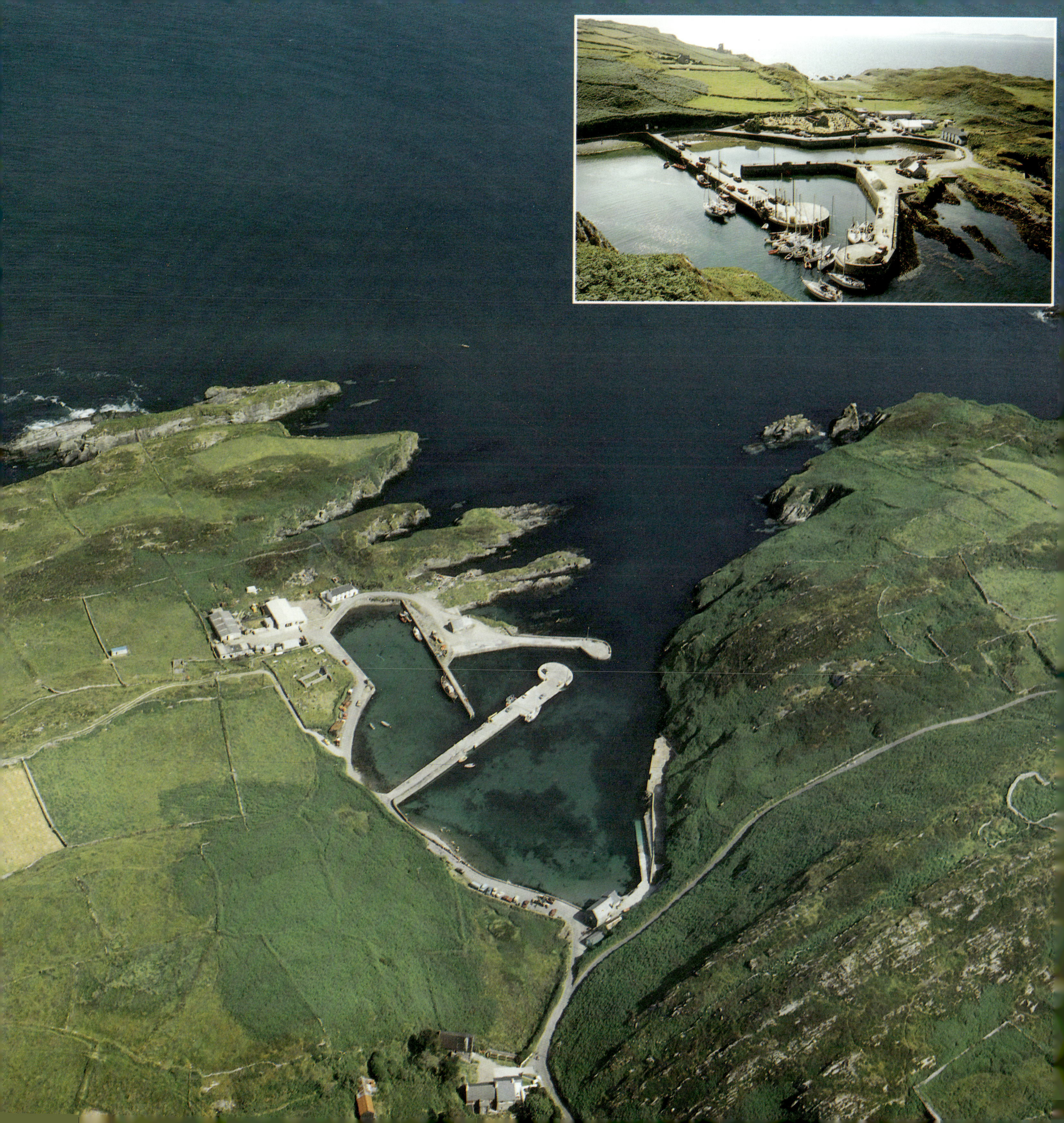

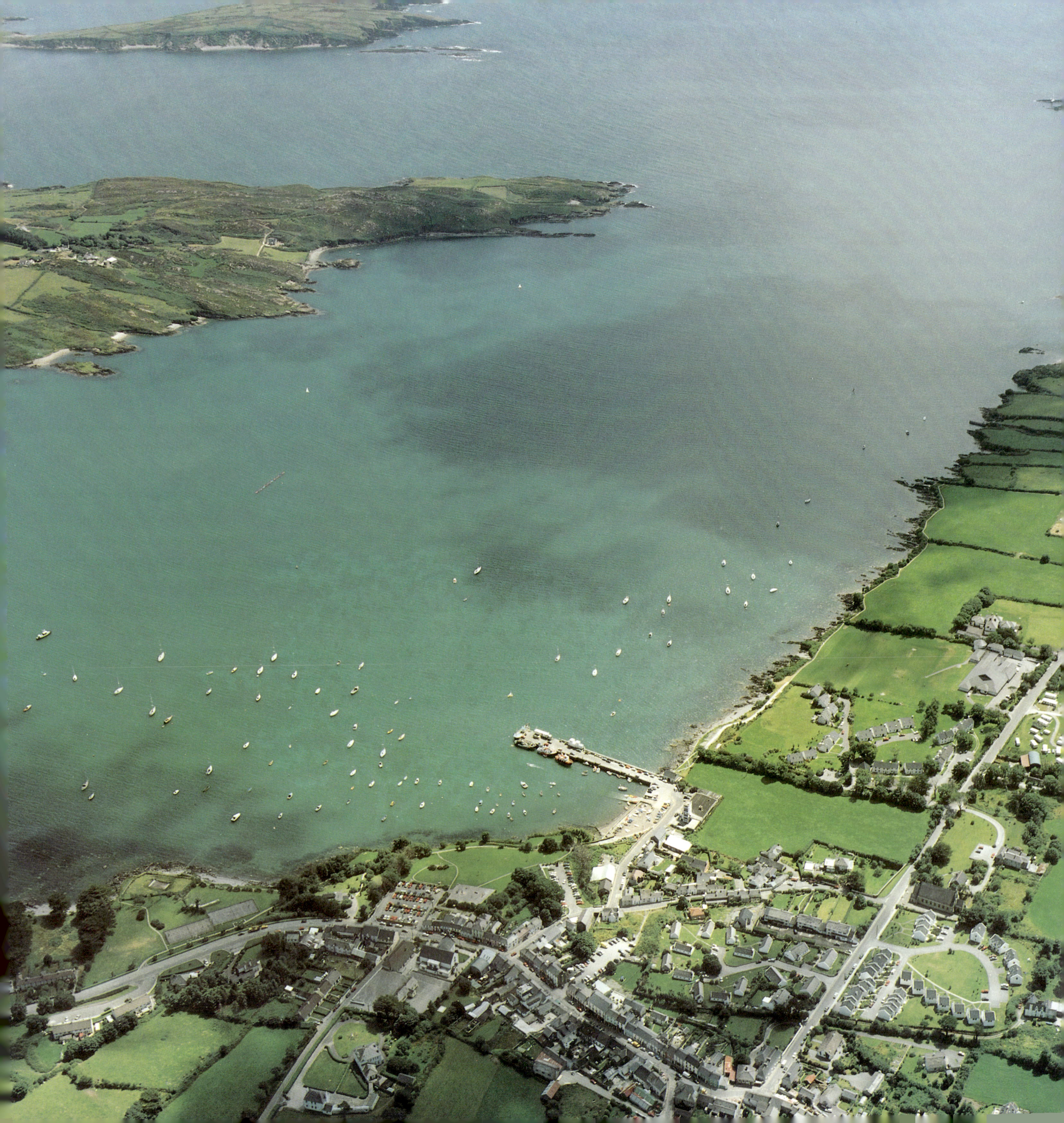

The village and harbour of Schull in west Cork and above,
'all the shades of blue', with the harbour full of visiting yachts in the summer of 1996.

A westerly view over Horse Island, Castle Island and Long Island in Roaring Water Bay
and right, looking back east for our American cousins,
Long Island, Long Island Sound and Coney Island.

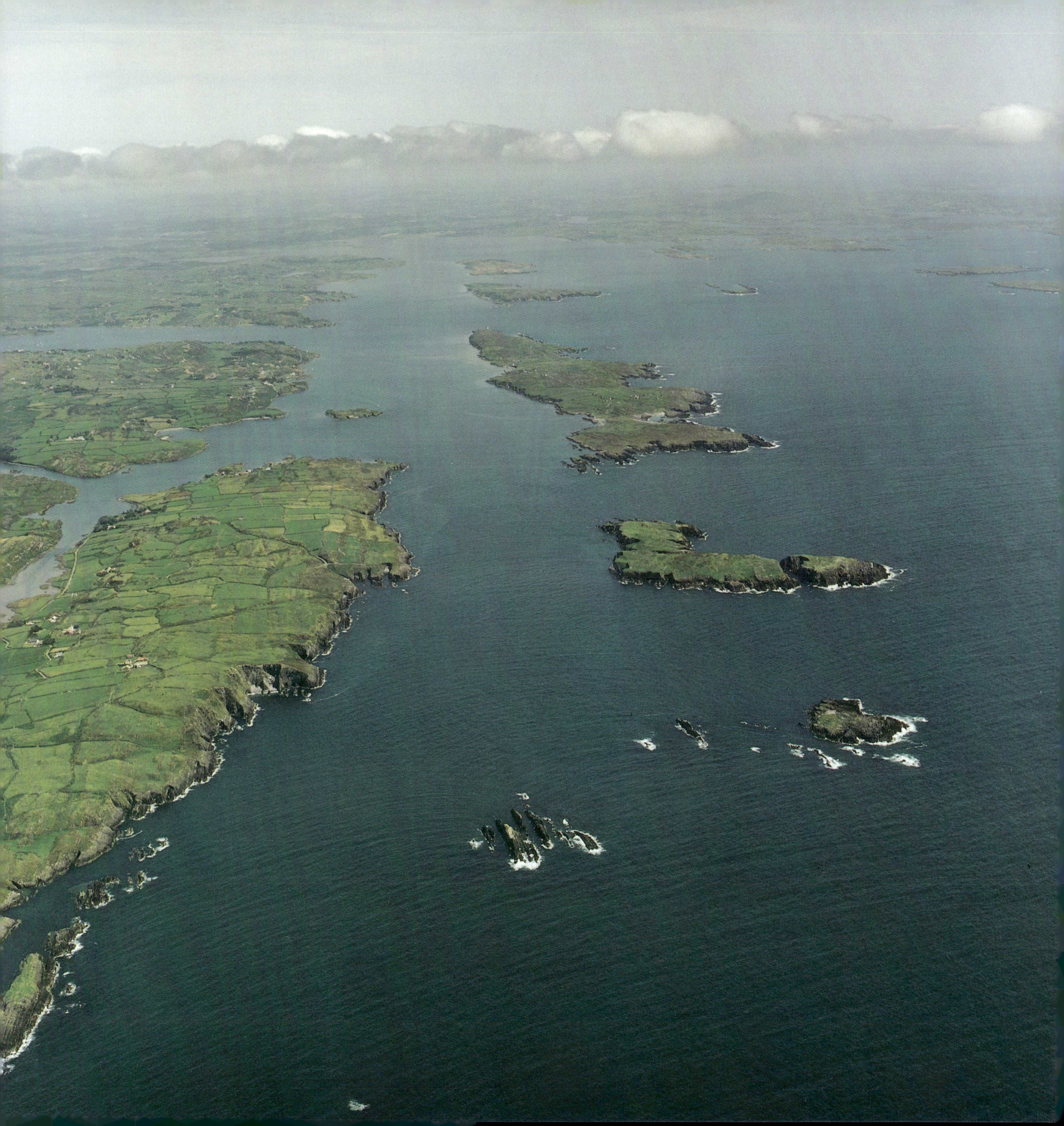

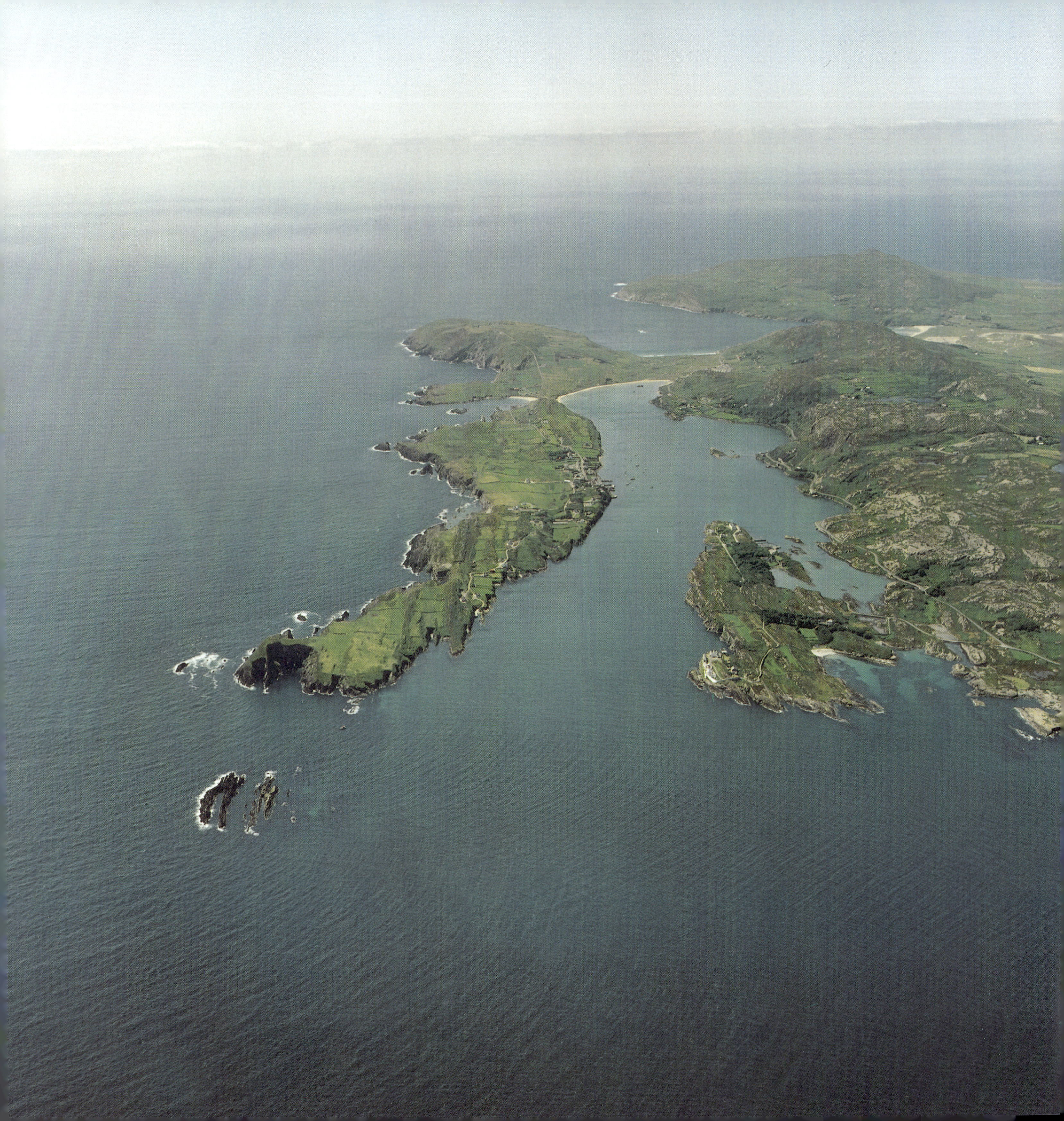

The safe and sheltered haven of Crookhaven with above,
the Fastnet Rock and Lighthouse. The south-west corner of Ireland
off the southern coast of County Cork.

The village of Durrus with Dunmanus Bay stretching to the west and the edges of west Cork. Right, the square in Bantry town with harbour and pier at the head of Bantry Bay.

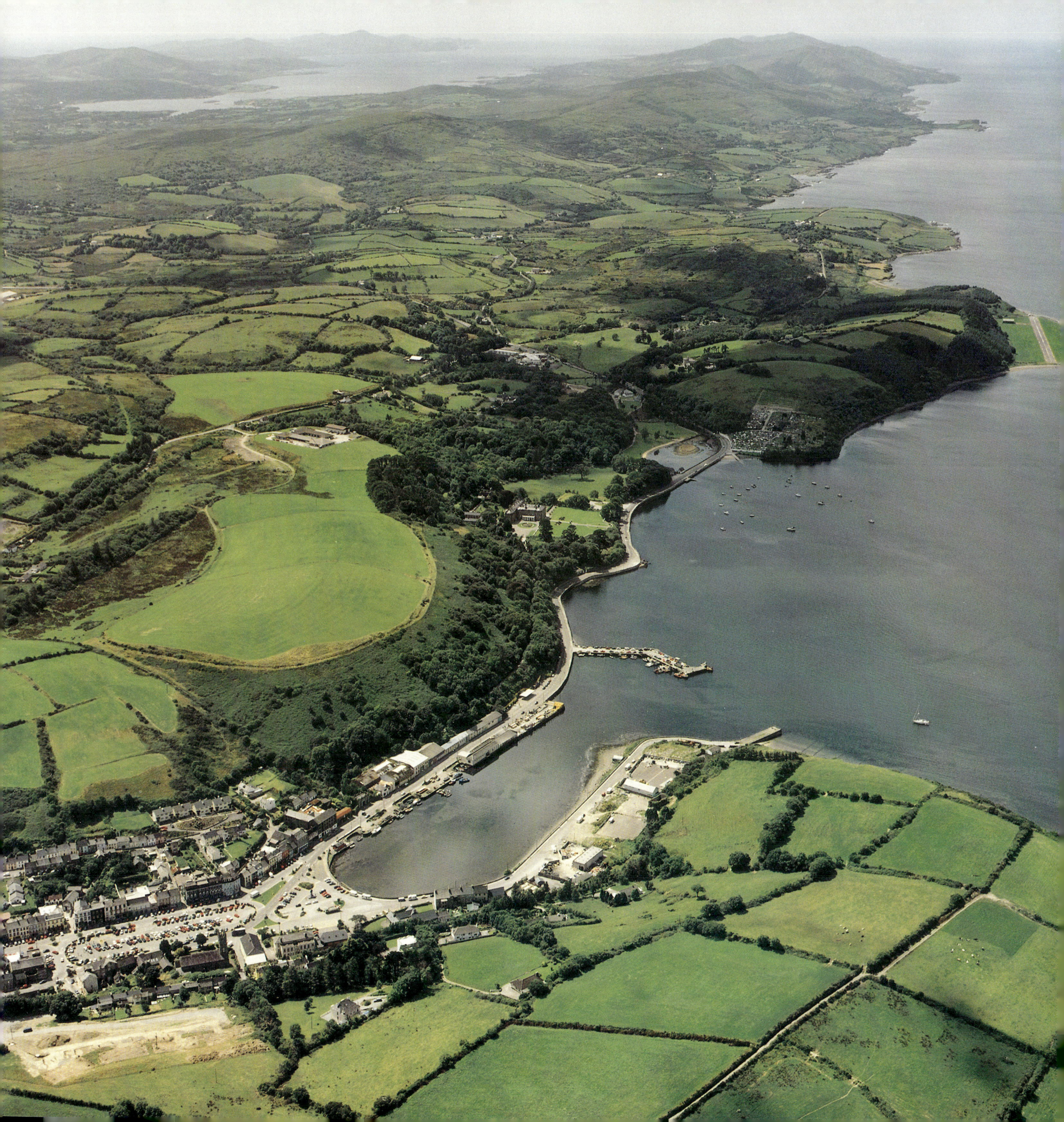

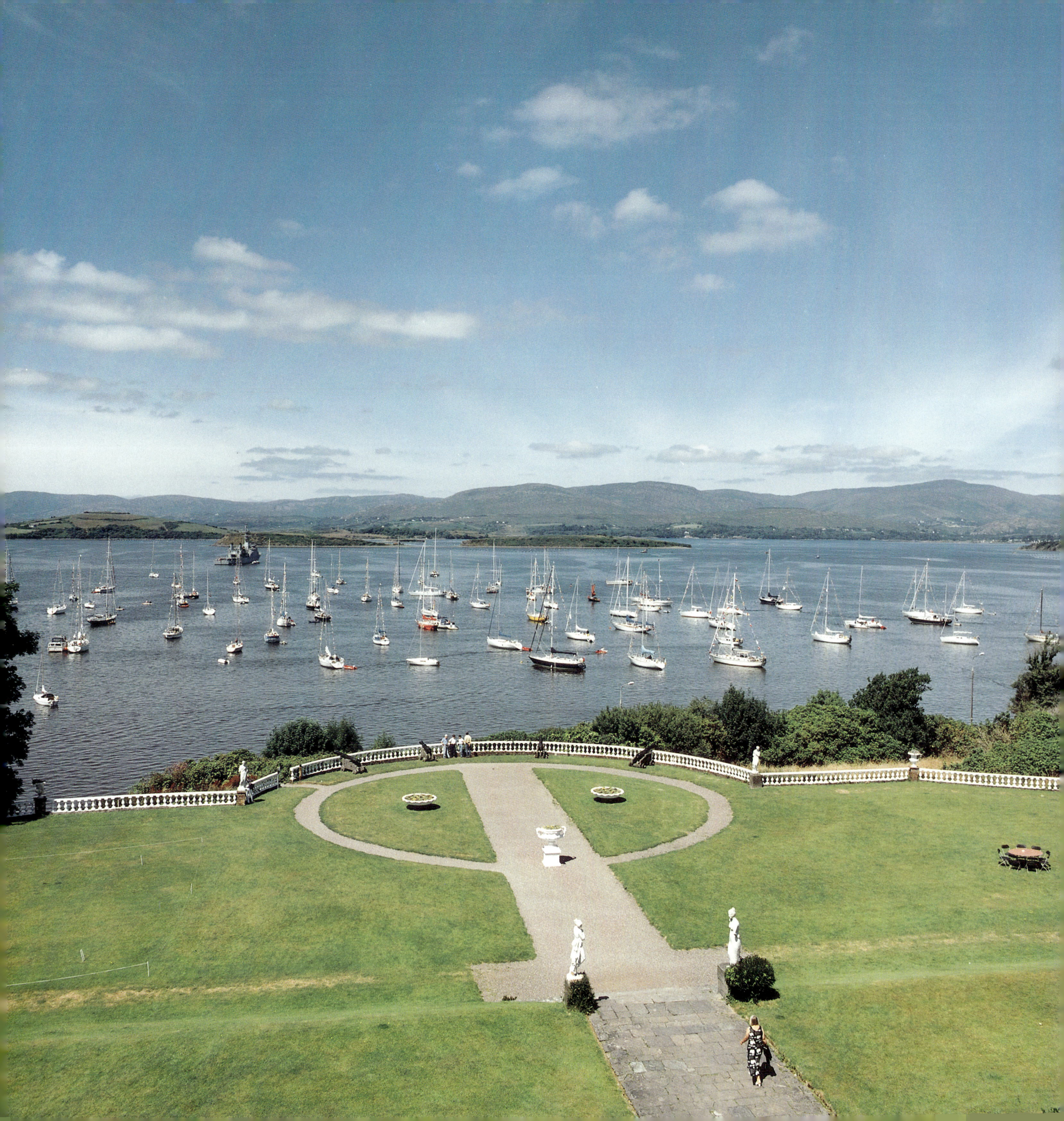

A sailing fleet viewed from the roof of Bantry House in July 1996, two hundred years after the French 'Non-Invasion' of Ireland of 1796. Above, a December view over Bantry and Whiddy Island to Glengarriff.

A view from the south-west into Glengarriff.
Right, Garinish Island and the Italian Garden's on the Gulf Stream
next to Glengarriff, County Cork.

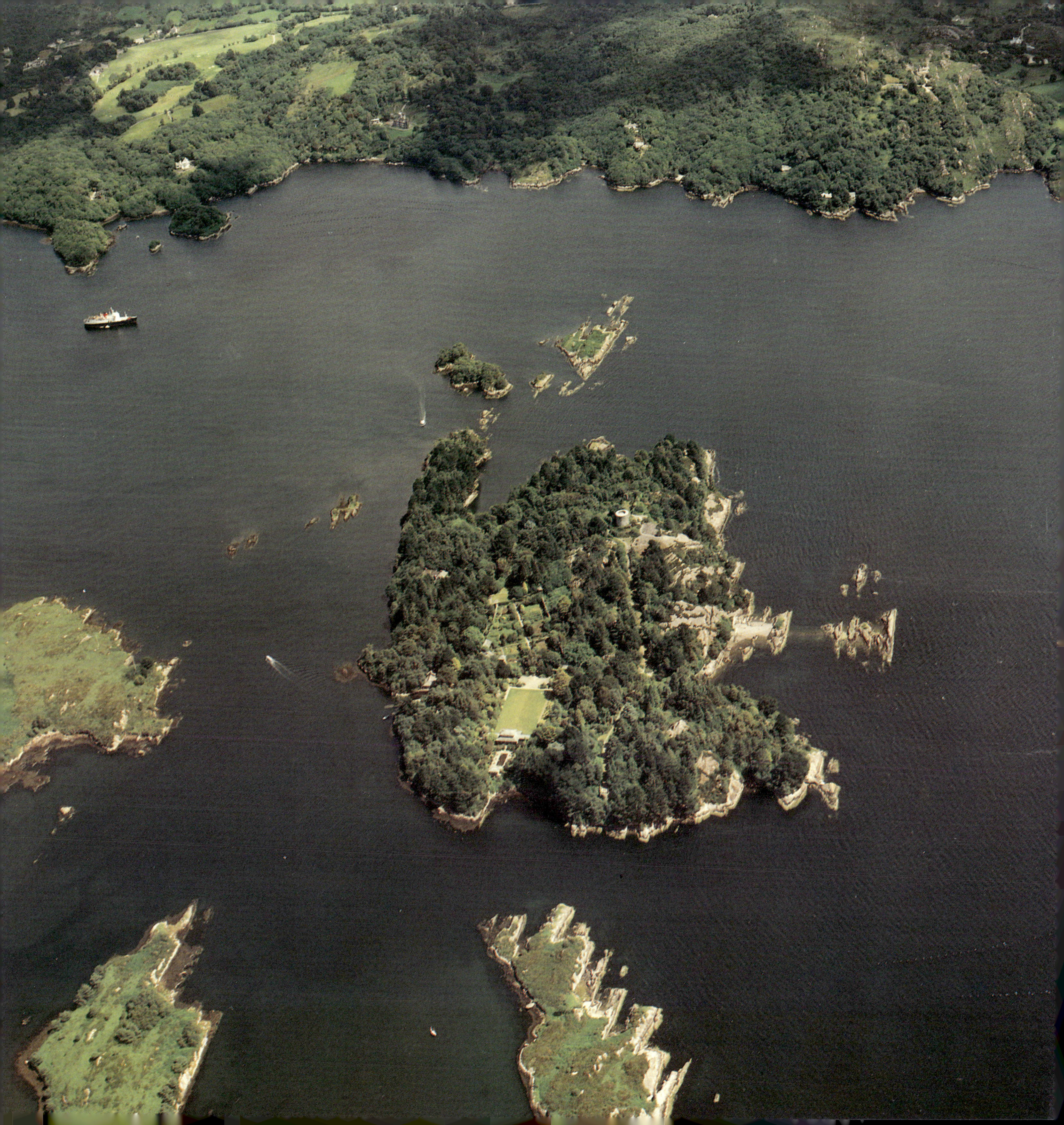

Above, the ruins of Dunboy House overlooking Dunboy Bay and Piper Sound. The larger photograph shows the Sound, with Bere Island on the right and the fishing port of Castletown Berehaven in the distance.

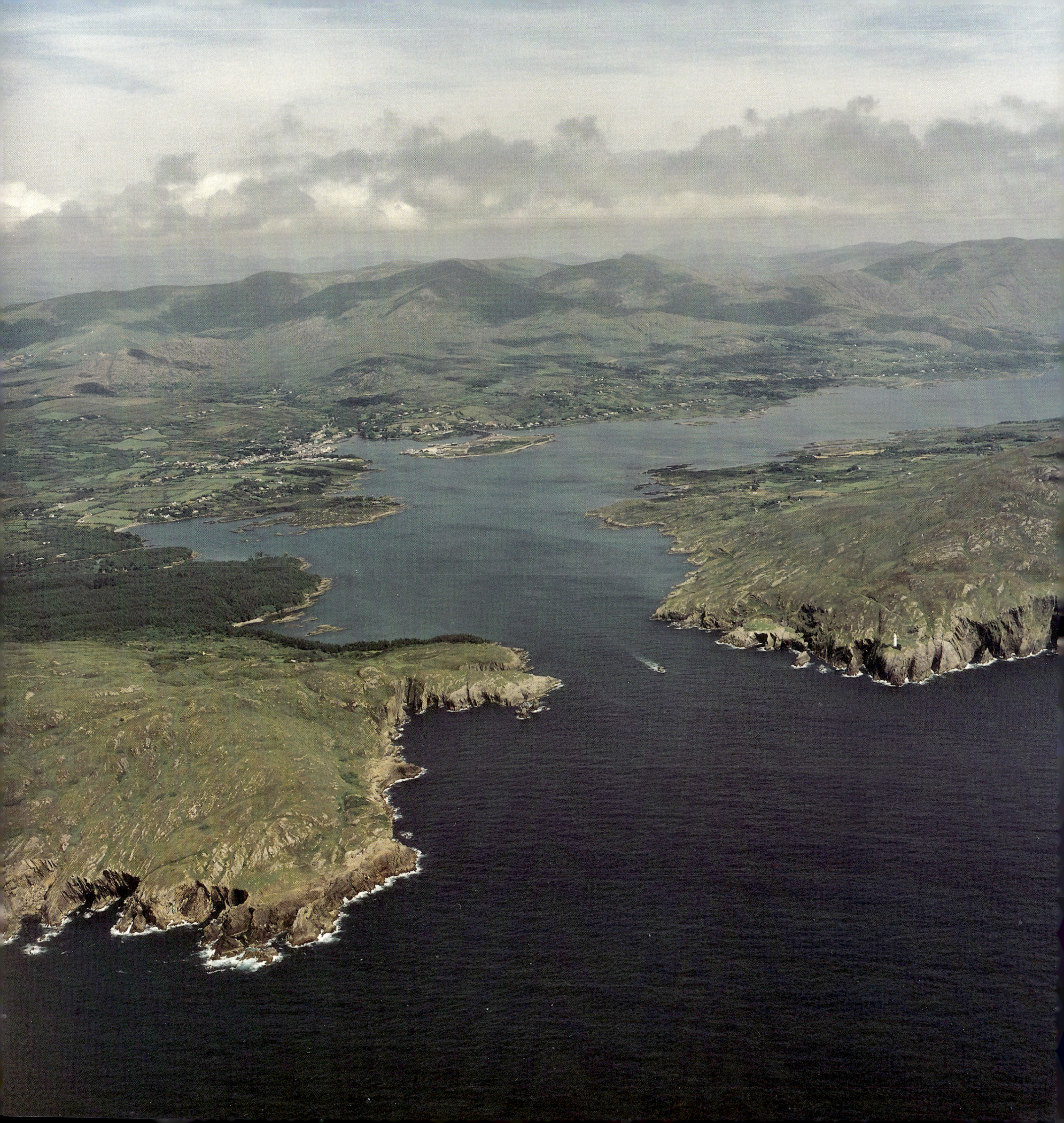

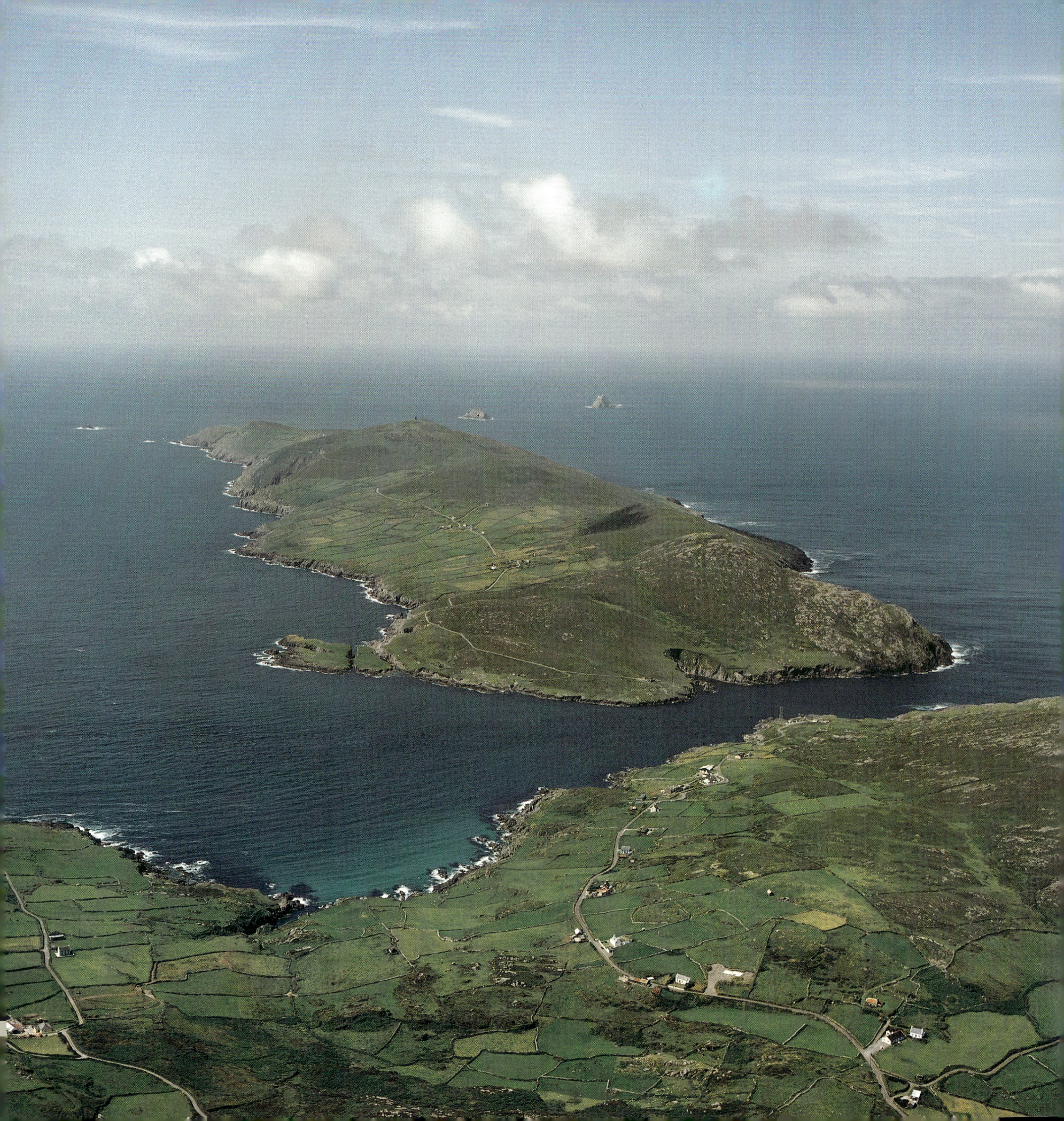

Dursey Island, joined to County Cork by a cablecar, with the Calf, the Cow and the Bull Rocks away to the west. Right, Bunaw Harbour within Kilmakilloge Harbour in County Kerry on the southern shore of the Kenmare River.

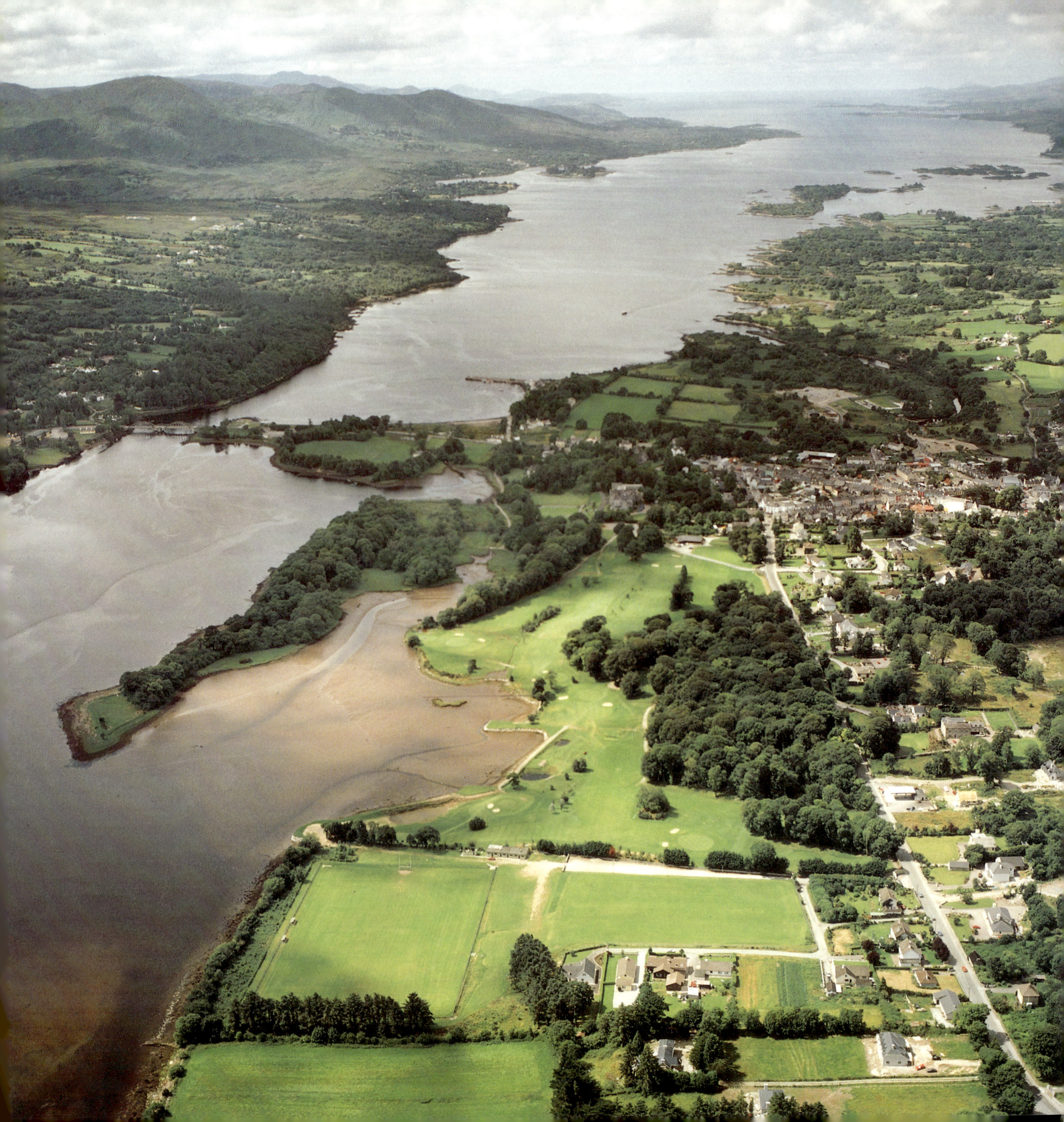

The town of Kenmare at the head of the Kenmare River in County Kerry and above, Sneem Harbour and Oysterbed Pier with the Sneem River winding away to the colourful village on the top right hand corner.

Deenish Island and Fish Farm with Scariff in the distance, four miles to the west of Derrynane and right, a spectacular view of Derrynane near Caherdaniel on the Ring of Kerry.

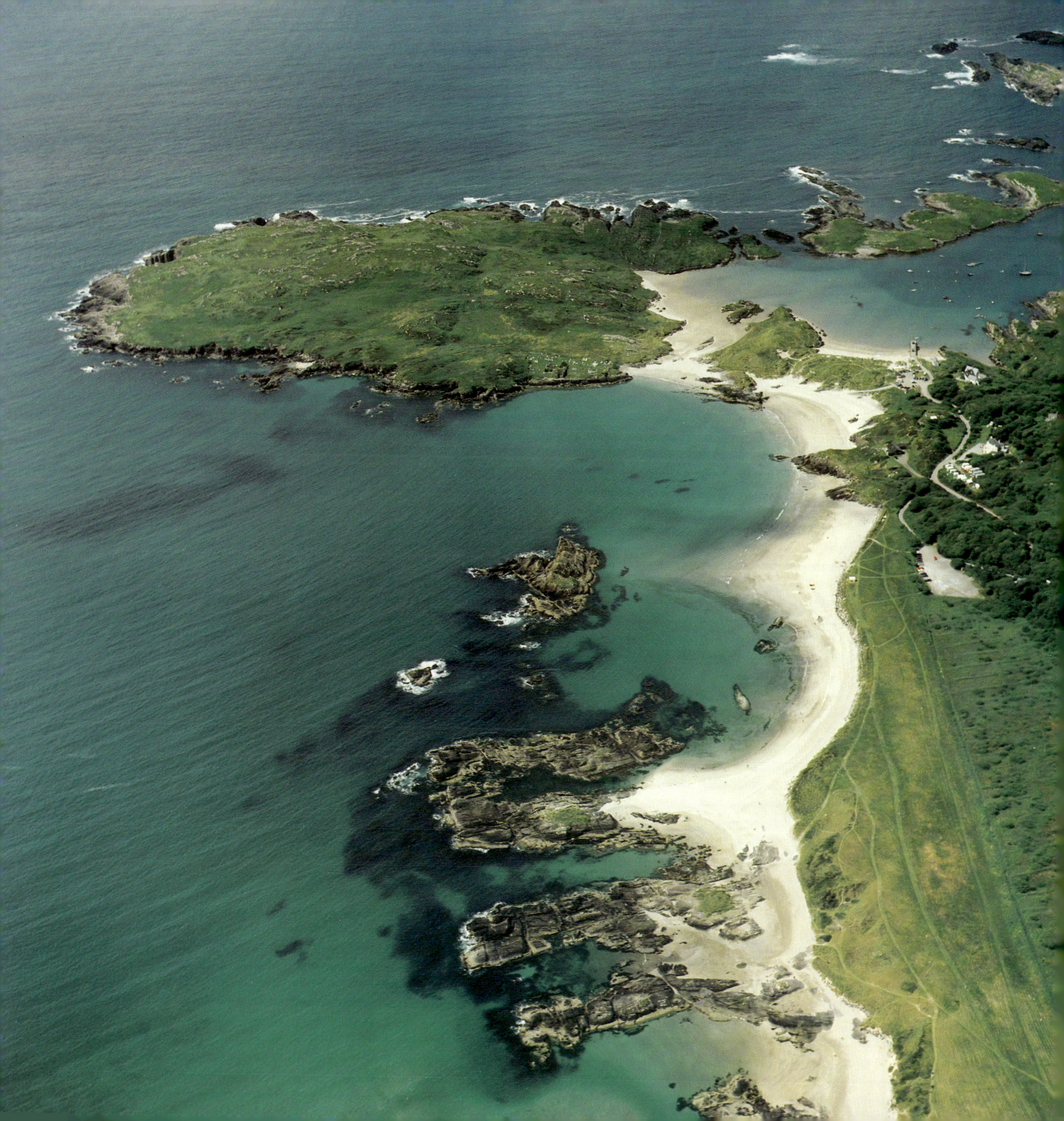

The steps leading up from the pier and right, the Beehive Huts dating from around 800 AD on the top of Skellig Michael off the coast of County Kerry.

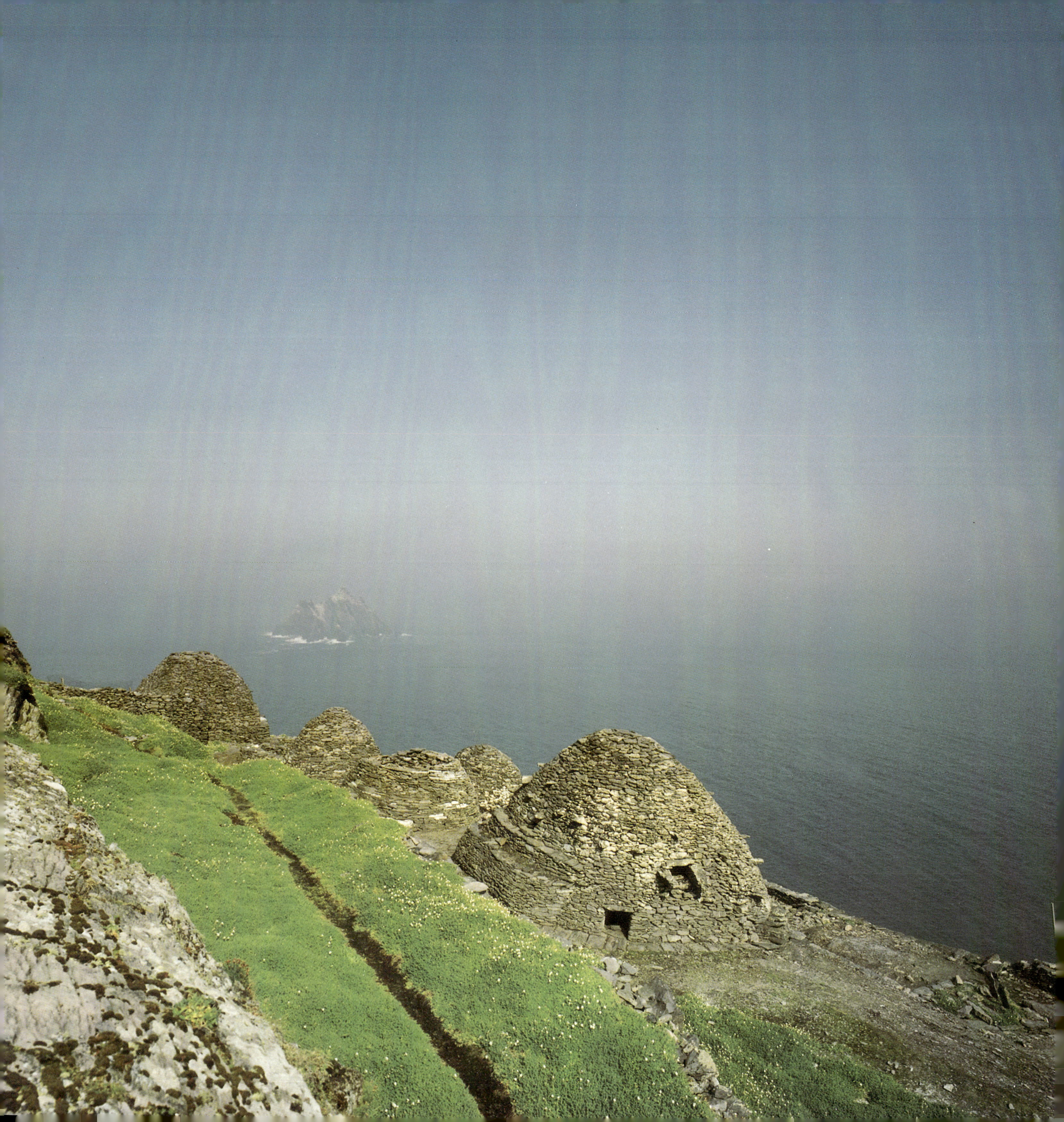

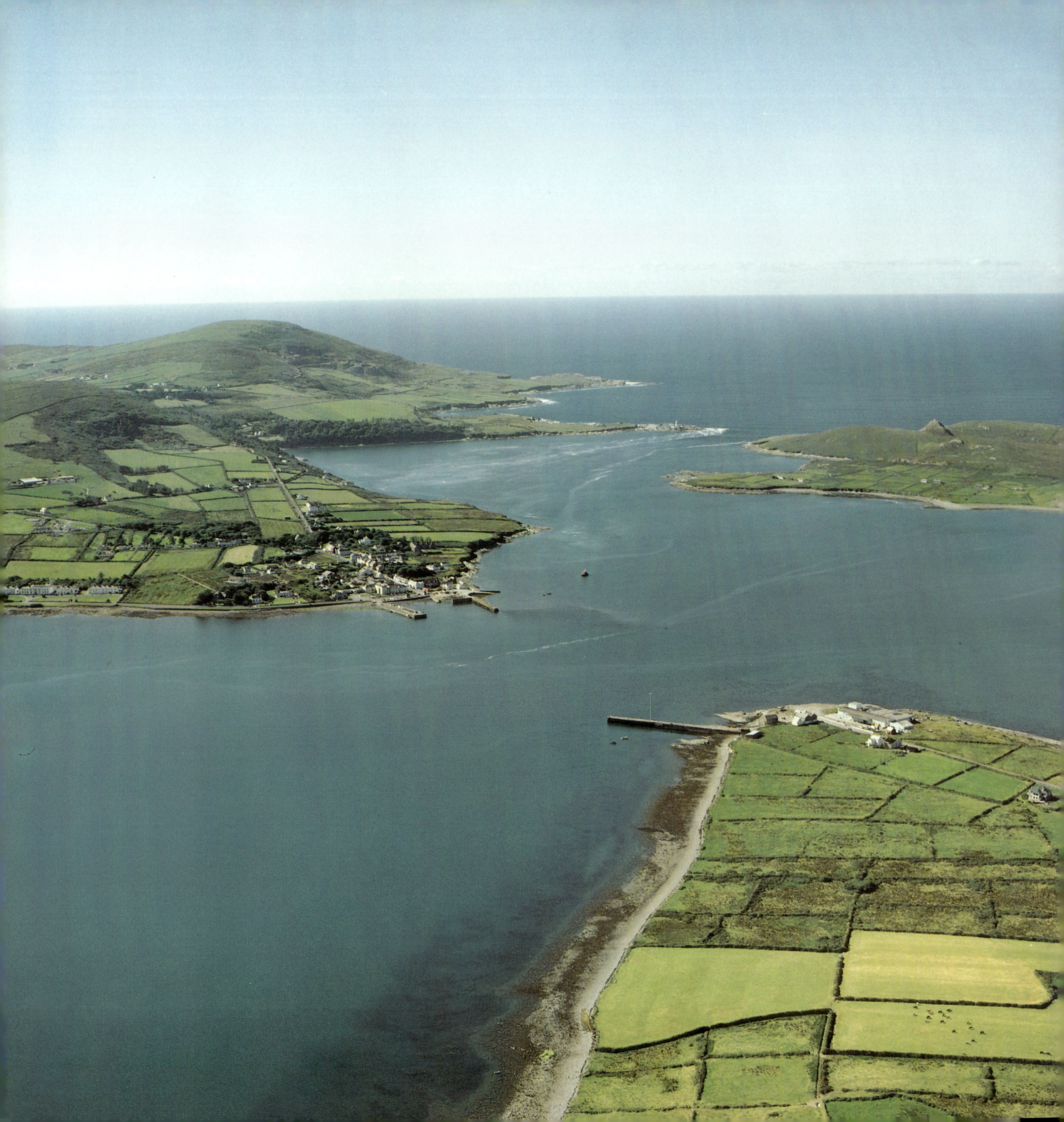

Reenard Point and Pier in the foreground looking towards Knightstown on Valentia Island. Above, the town of Cahersiveen on the Ring of Kerry.

The Bay and Golf Club at Dooks near Glenbeigh
and right, Inch Strand on Dingle Bay, stretching as far as the eye can see.

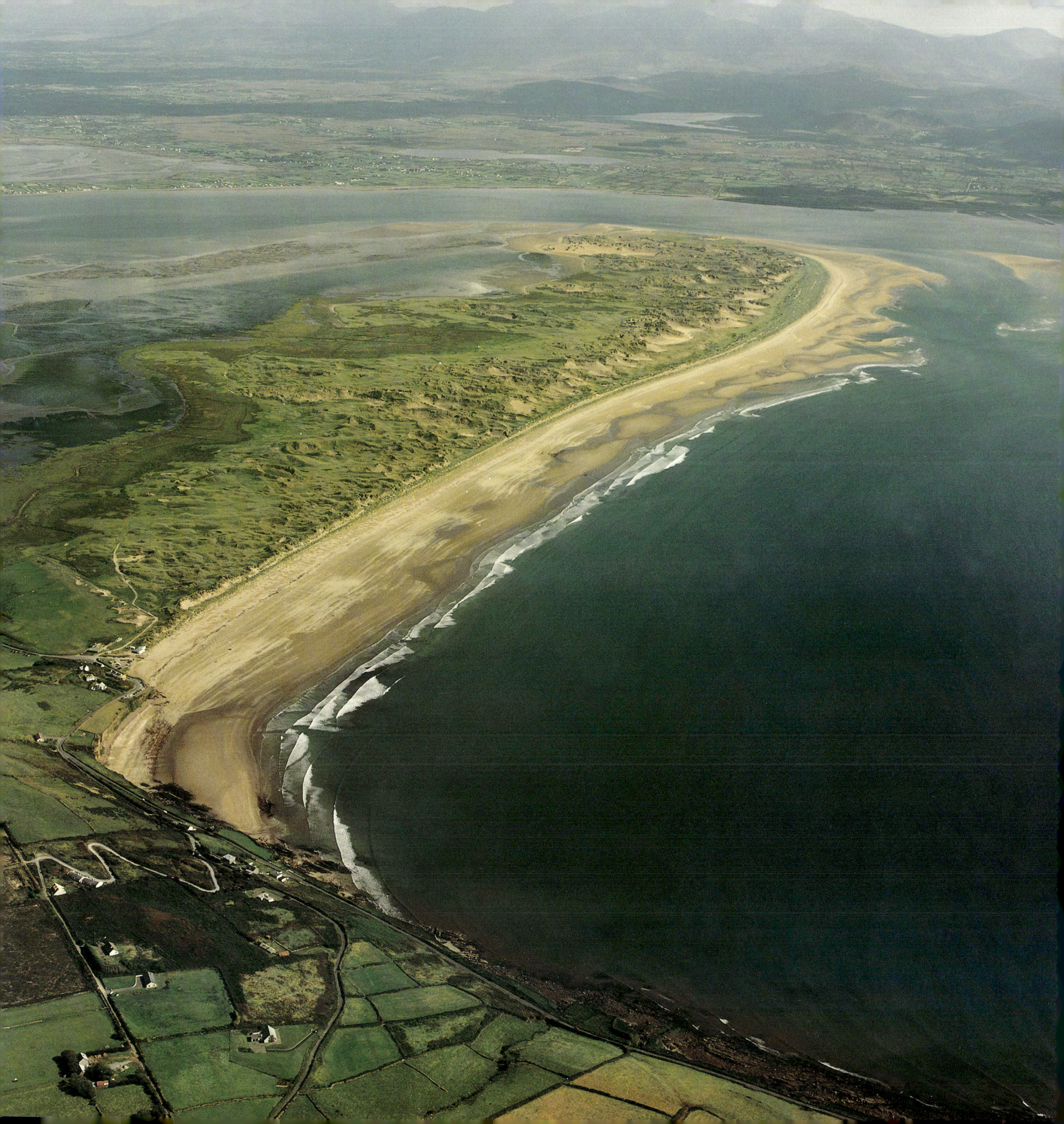

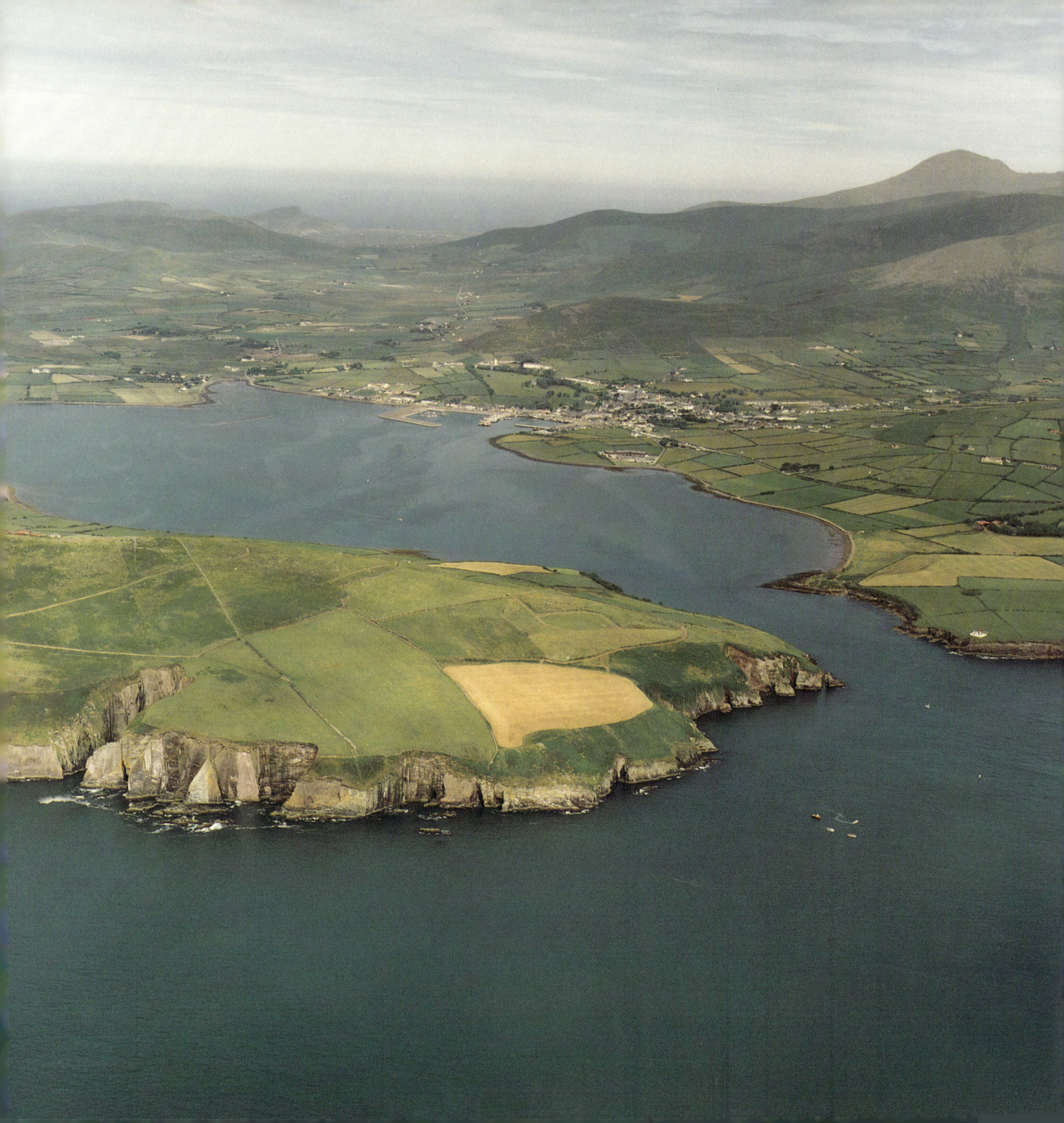

Boats surrounding 'Fungie' the dolphin, just at the entrance to Dingle Harbour and above, Dingle town in Kerry surrounded by mountains with the Magharee Islands just visible over the Conor Pass.

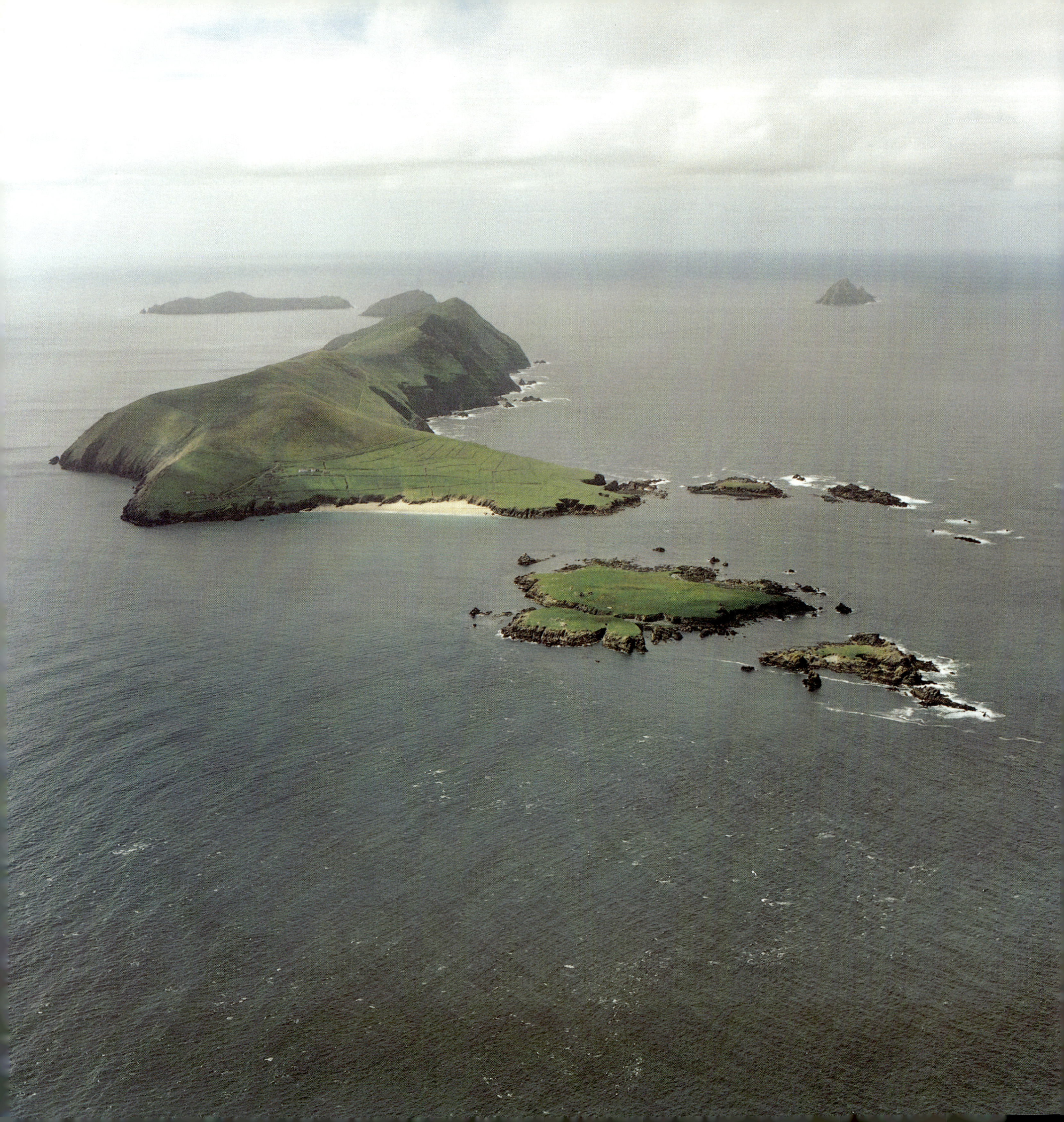

The Blasket Islands to the west of the Dingle peninsula.
Above, Fenit, the port for Tralee, the capital of Kerry.

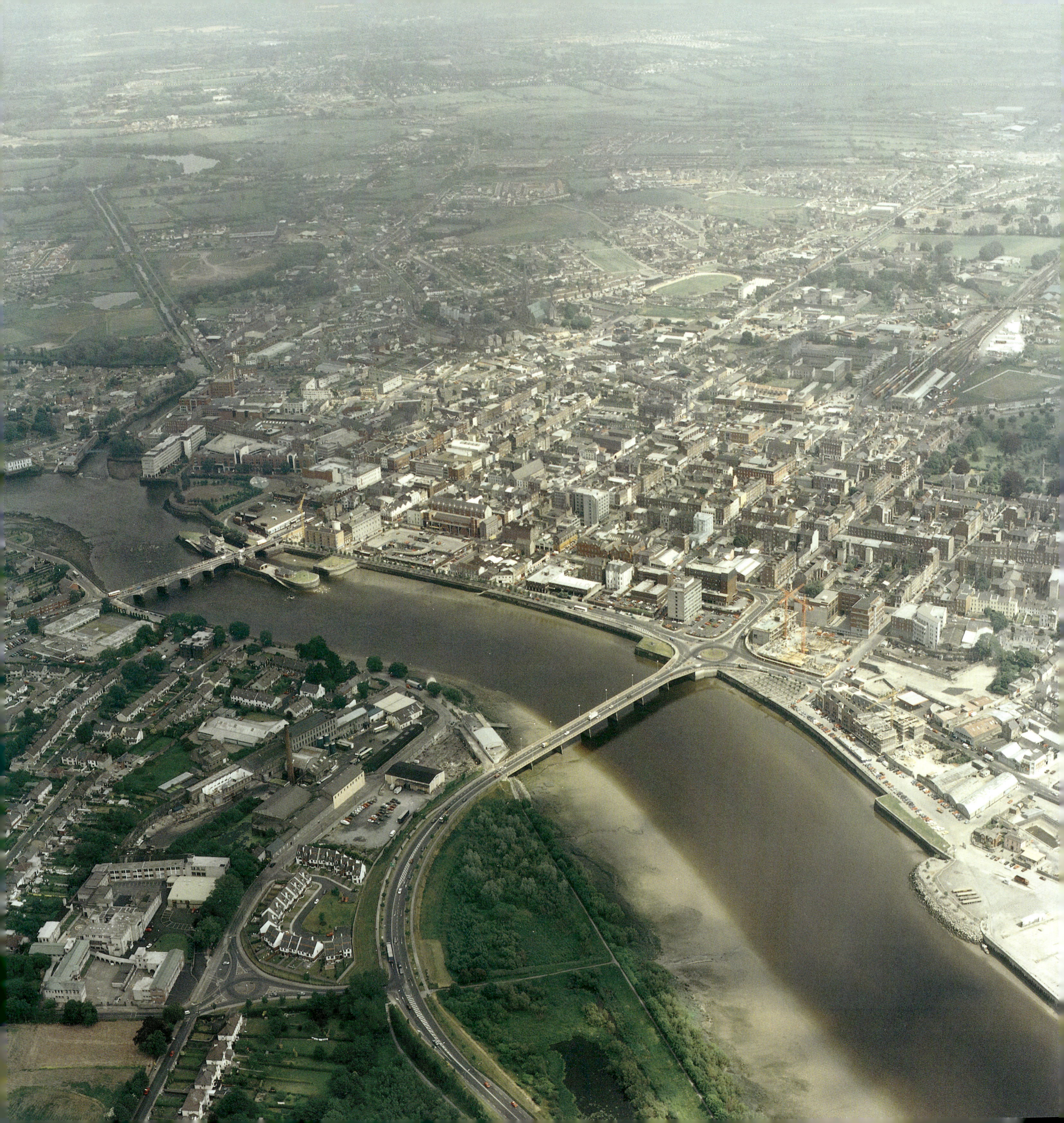

Limerick city and above, the mighty River Shannon as it meanders
past Killaloe on its way to Limerick and the Atlantic Ocean.

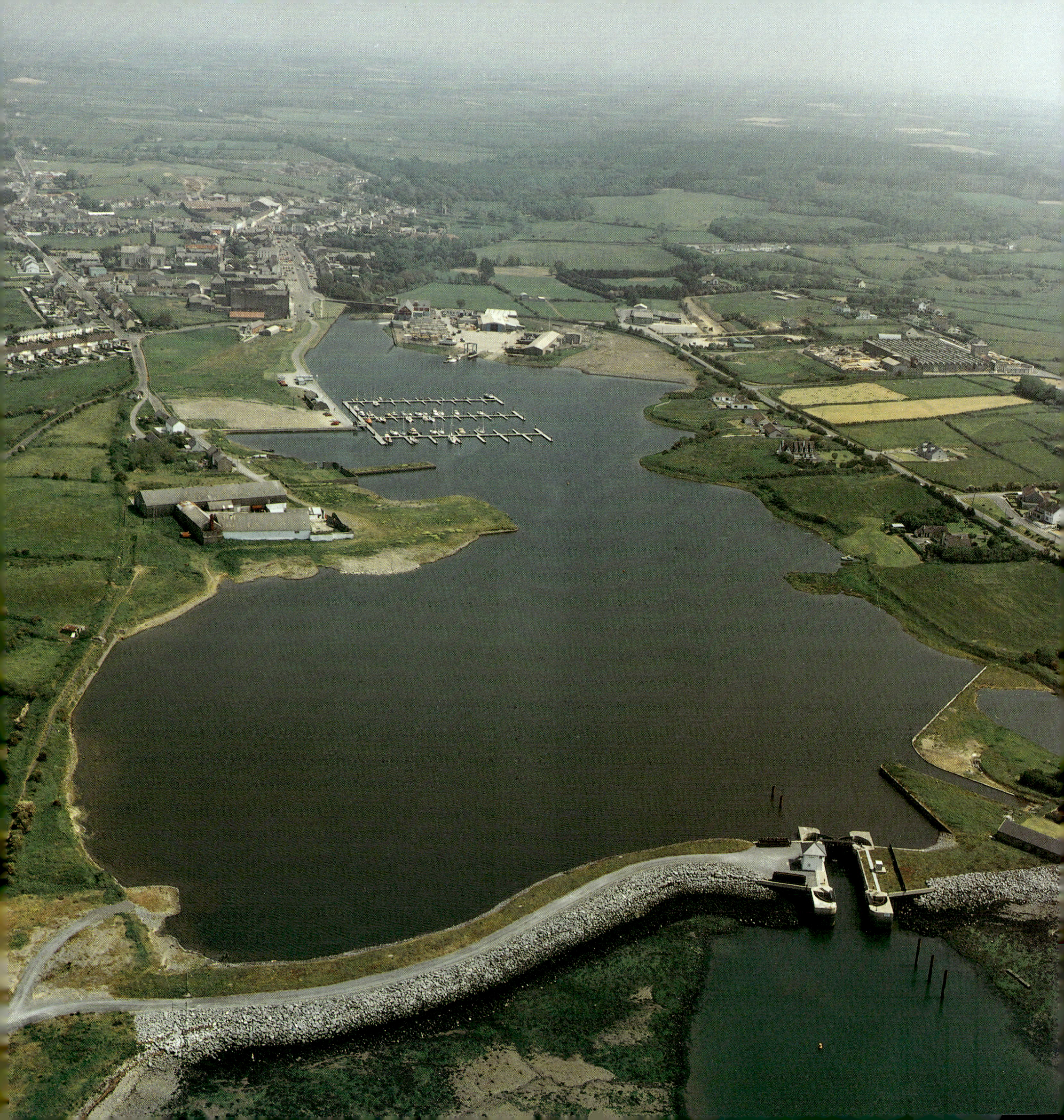

Kilrush Creek with lock gates and marina.
Above, pier and castle with the village of Carrigaholt in the distance.

The popular seaside resort of Kilkee on the coast of County Clare and right, the rugged splendour of the Cliffs of Moher on the border of the Atlantic Ocean.

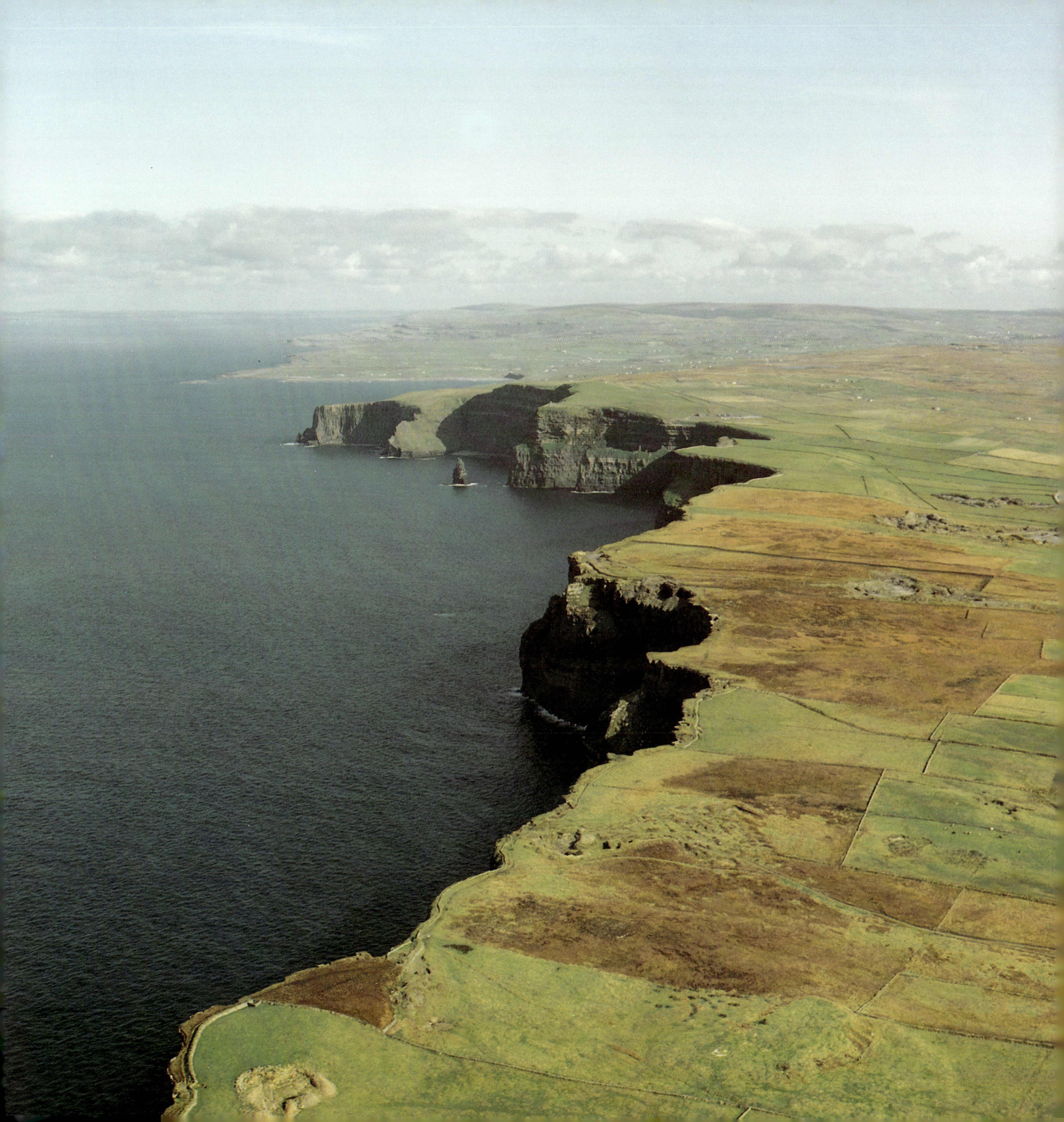

Ballyvaughan village on the north shore of County Clare.

Progressing around the coastline of Ireland, we come to Connacht and fly around the edges of Galway Bay, starting over the village of Kinvara and Dunguaire Castle. We fly north past Rinville before arriving over Galway city on the River Corrib. From here we fly west over Spiddal and Rossaveal and sweep out to the south over the Aran Islands. Here, time stops for a while as we look down on a patchwork of stone walls, small fields, rock, cliffs and finally the fort at Dun Aengus on Inishmore.

Continuing north and then back over the edge of the Atlantic Ocean, we fly over the many bays that lead us towards Roundstone and Clifden, from where we have a great view of the Twelve Bens of Connemara. We head up the coast and fly out to the island of Inishbofin and then back east towards Killary Harbour, Ireland's only fjord and then back north to Achill Island, Blacksod Bay and the Mayo coast. We continue east past Rossport and Killala before reaching Rosses Point in Sligo Bay.

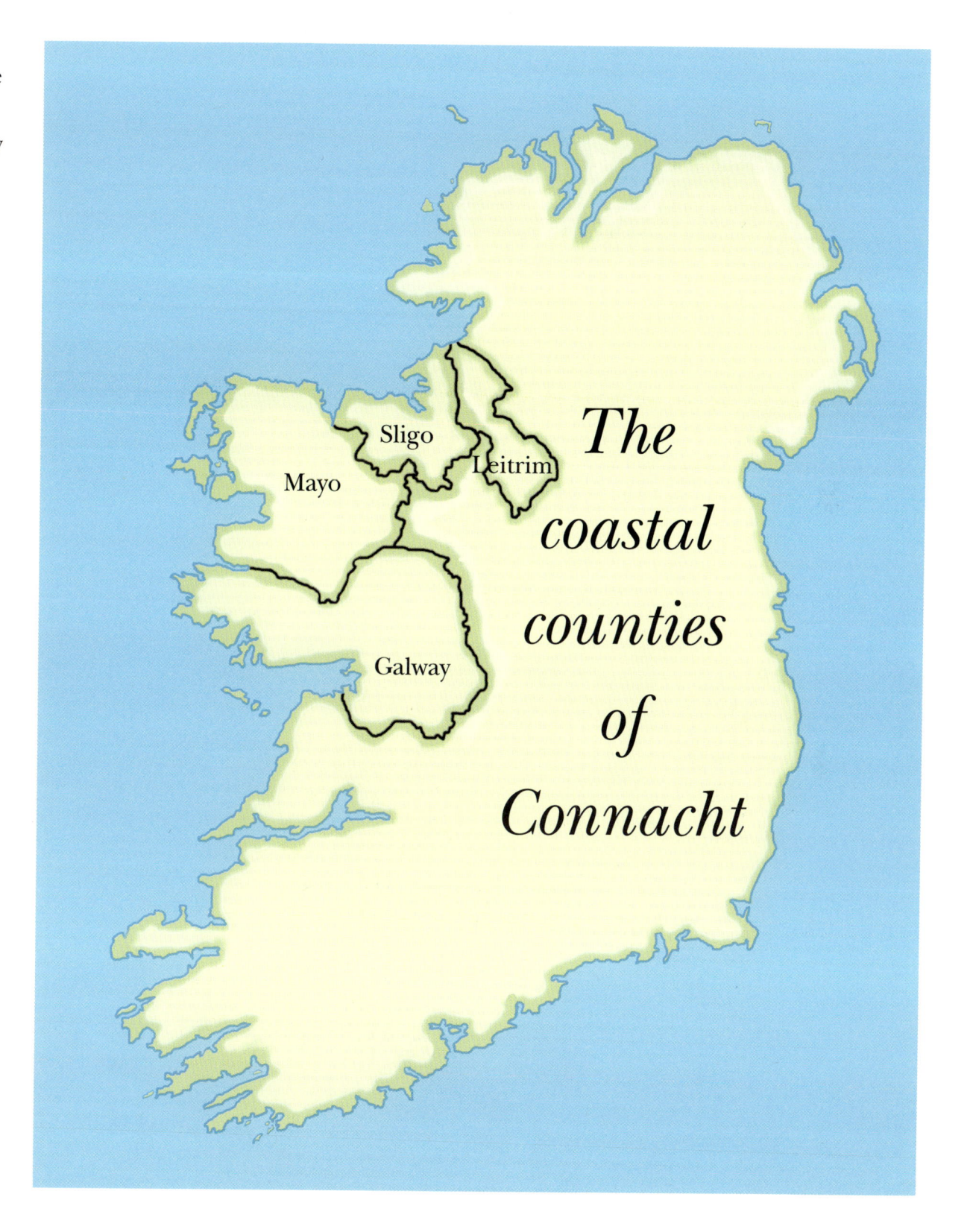

The coastal counties of Connacht

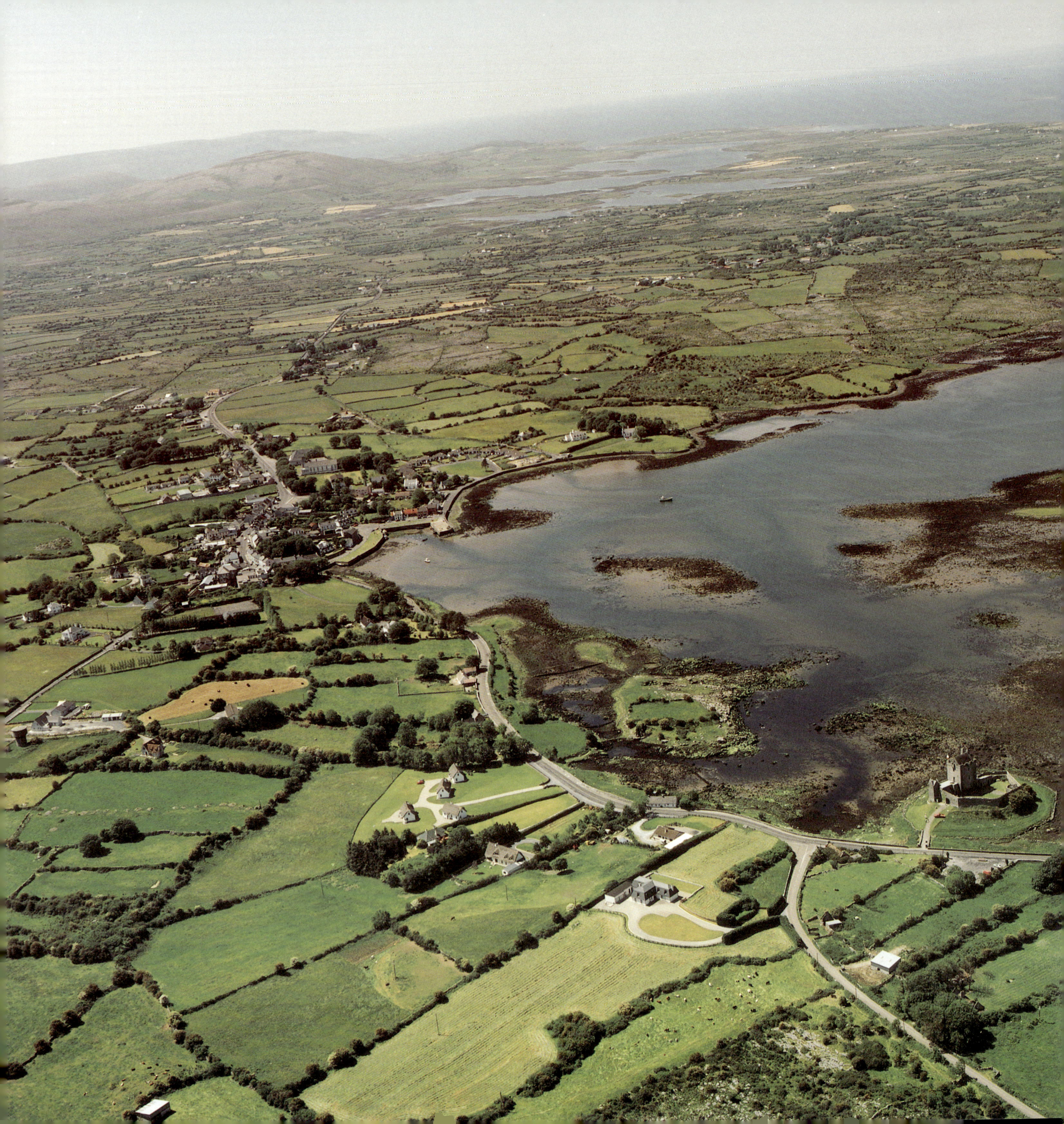

Kinvara village on the shore of Galway Bay with Dunguaire Castle to the bottom right of the picture and above, New Harbour, Rinville, home of Galway Bay Sailing Club.

Galway, the 'City of the Tribes', viewed above from the north and to the right from the south-west, a city with a charm of its own.

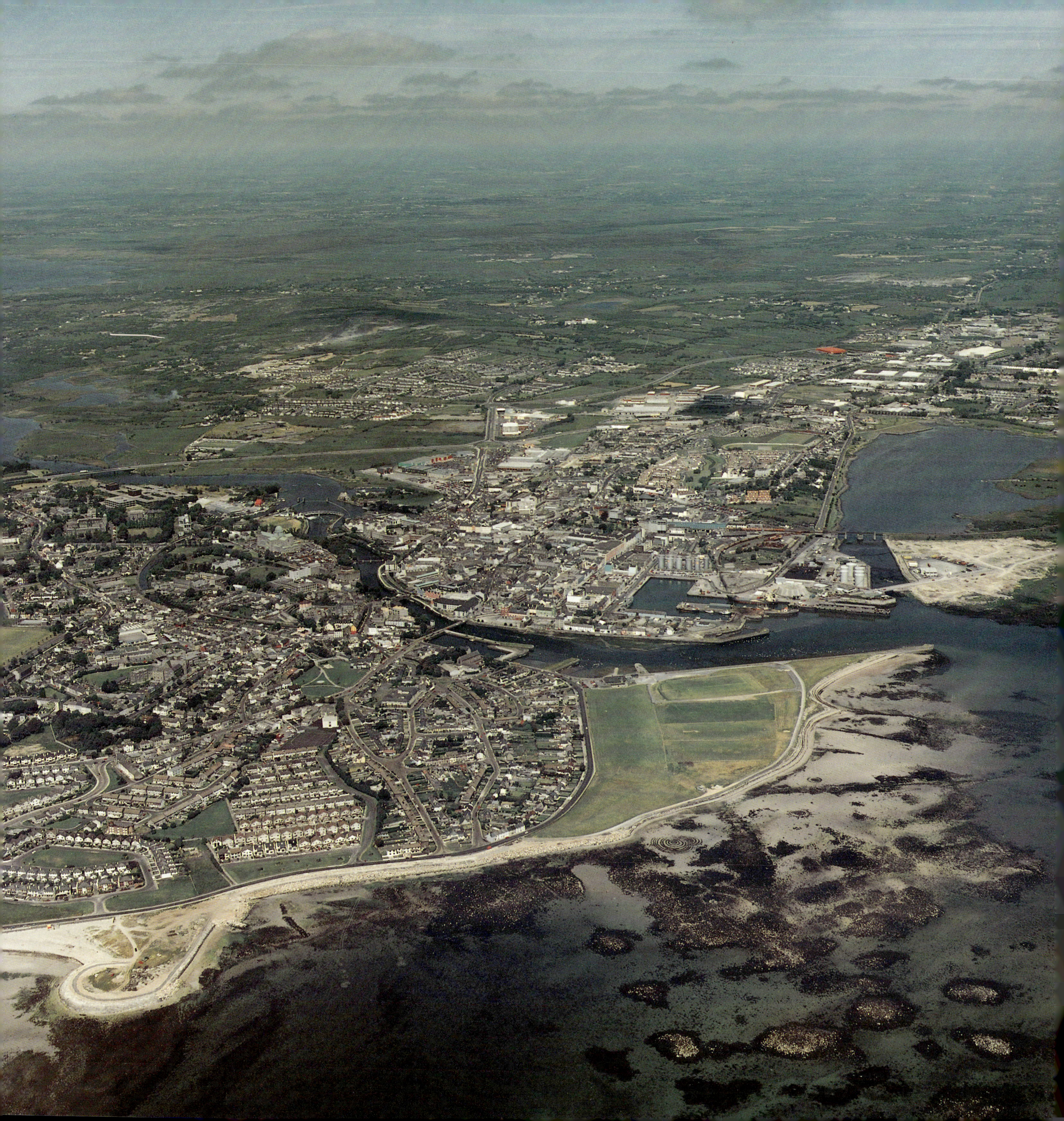

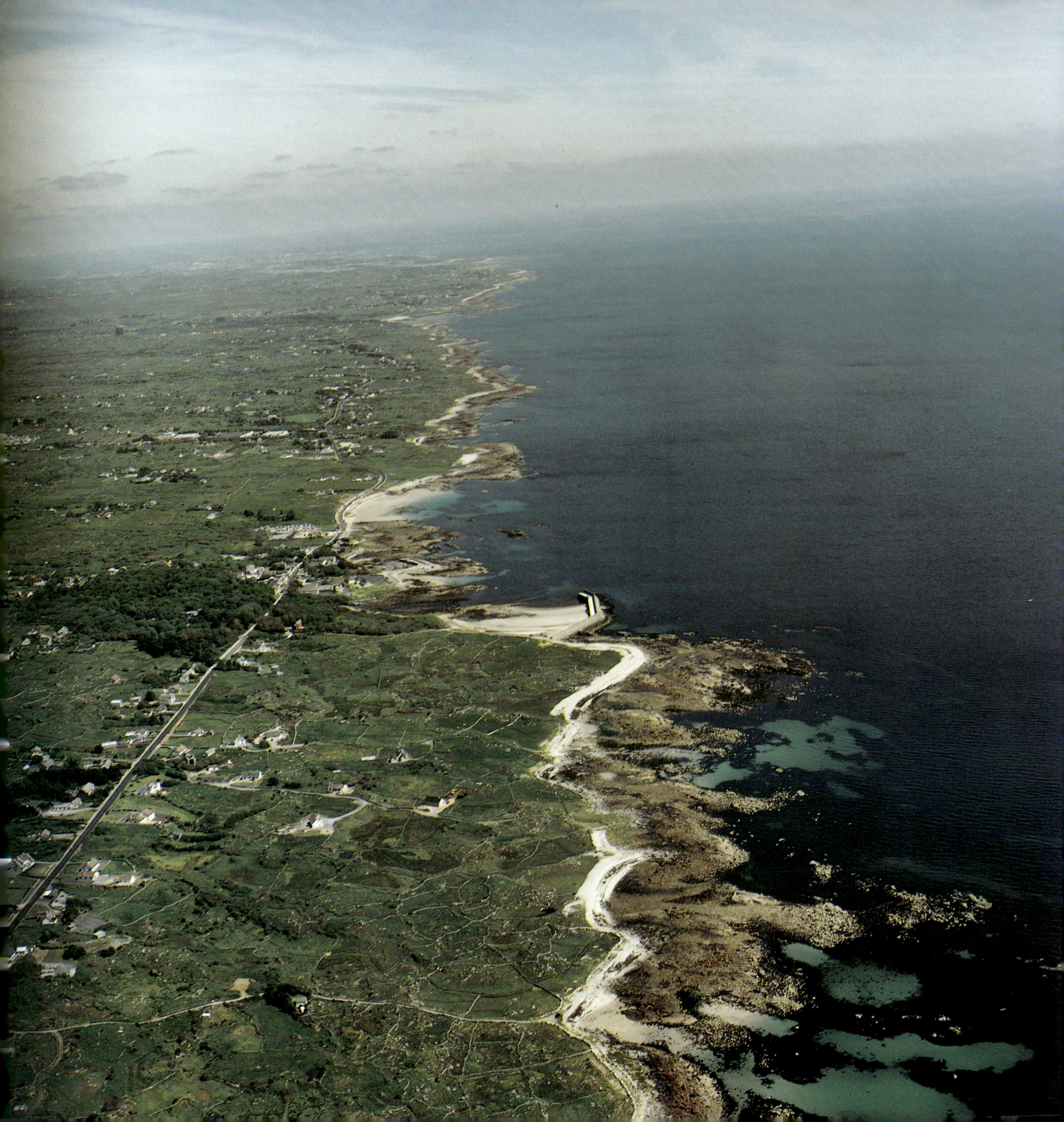

Spiddal, stretching along the north shore of Galway Bay
and above, Rossaveal, gateway to the Aran Islands.

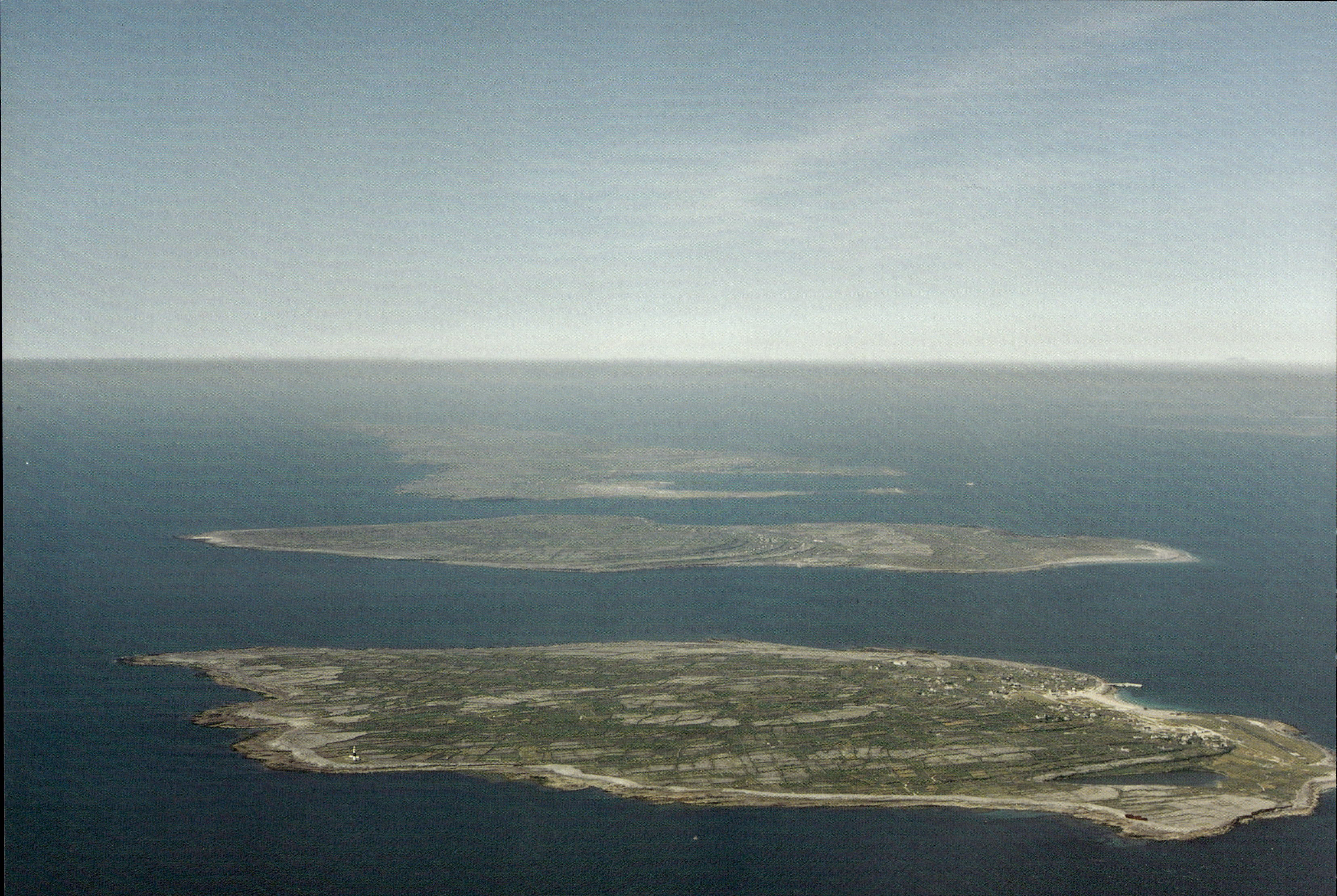

The Aran Islands - Inisheer, Inishmaan and Inishmore - viewed from the east and above, the stone walls and patchwork of fields on Inishmaan.

Inishmore, the south shore, looking north towards Kilronan and right, the fort of Dun Aengus perched on the cliff edge.

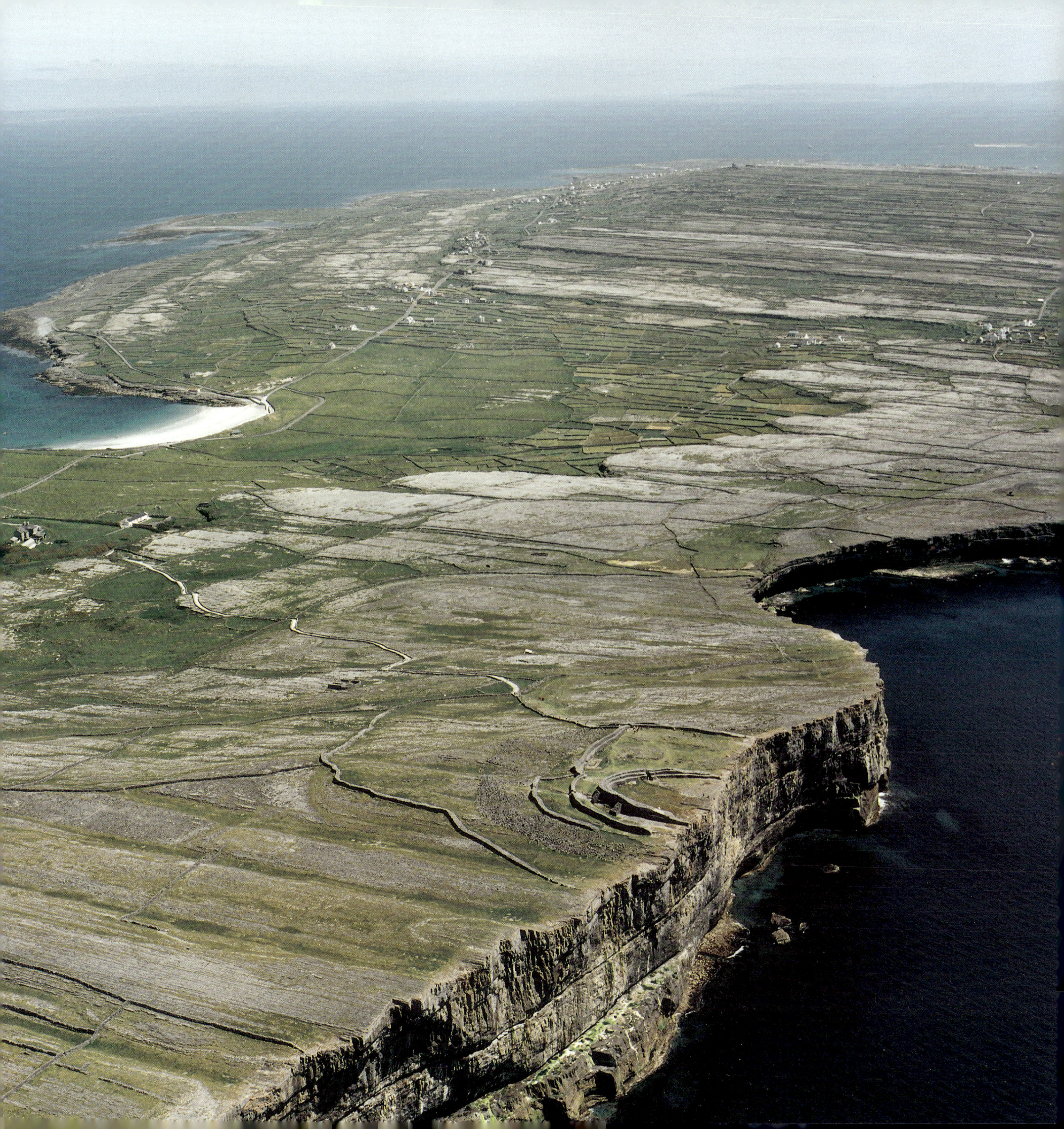

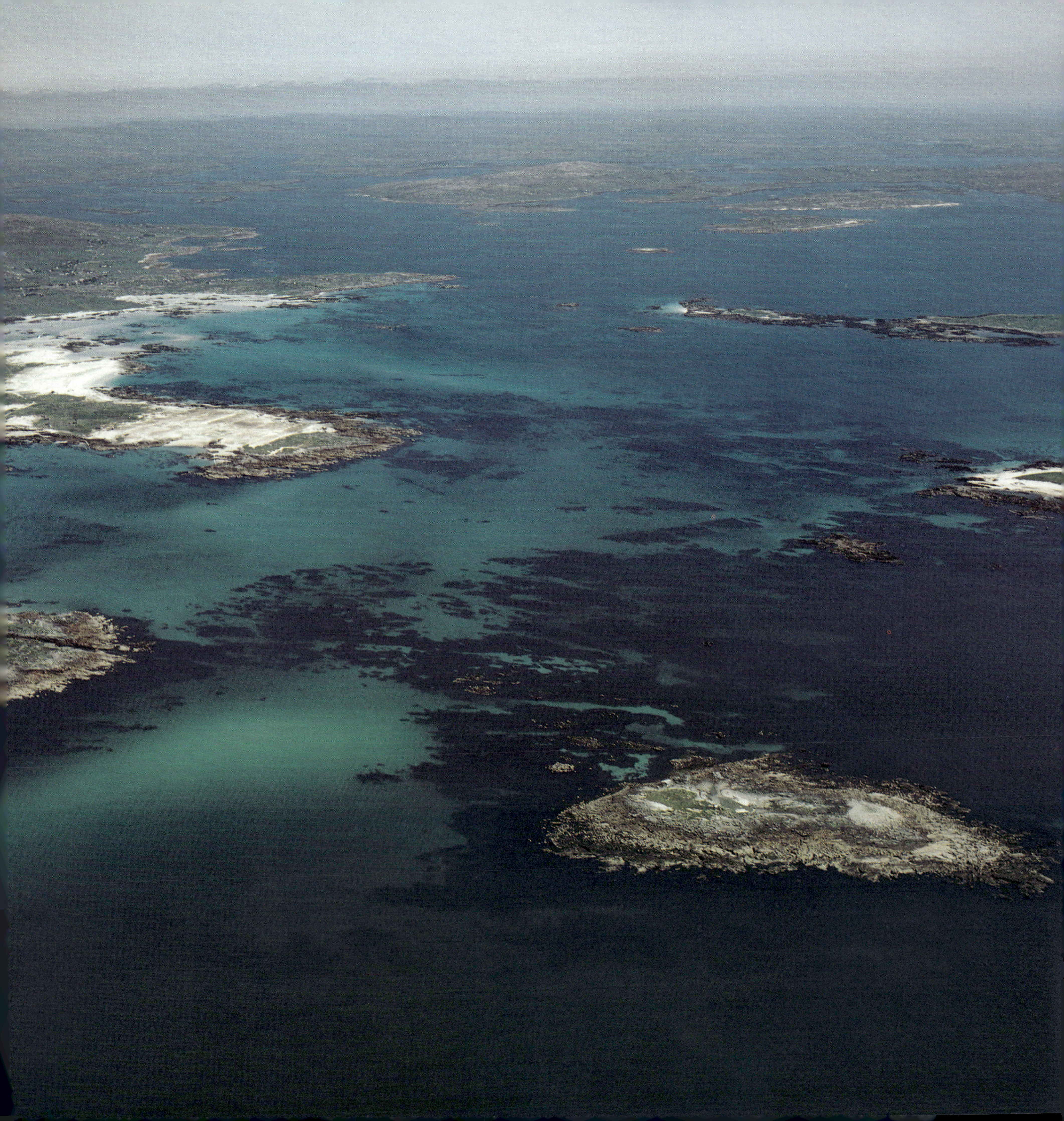

Ardmore Point with almost Caribbean colours at the start of Kilkieran Bay
which stretches 14 miles (23km) into the heart of Connemara
and above, the pier at Kilkieran Cove.

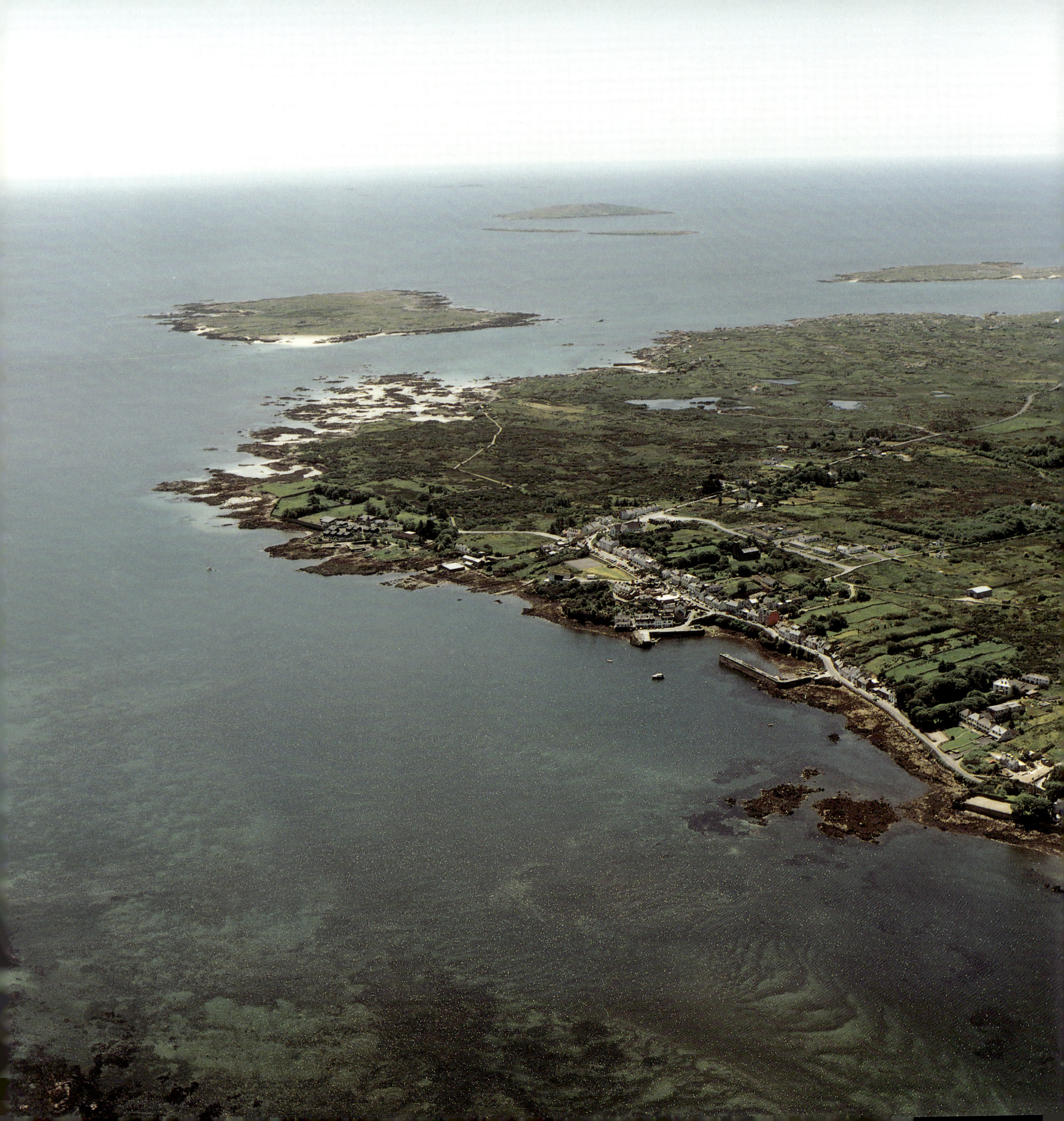

The fishing village of Roundstone leading to the glorious sandy beaches above, of Gorteen Bay with Dog's Bay close by on the right hand side.

Clifden Bay viewed from the east and right,
Clifden village with a backdrop of the
Twelve Bens of Connemara.

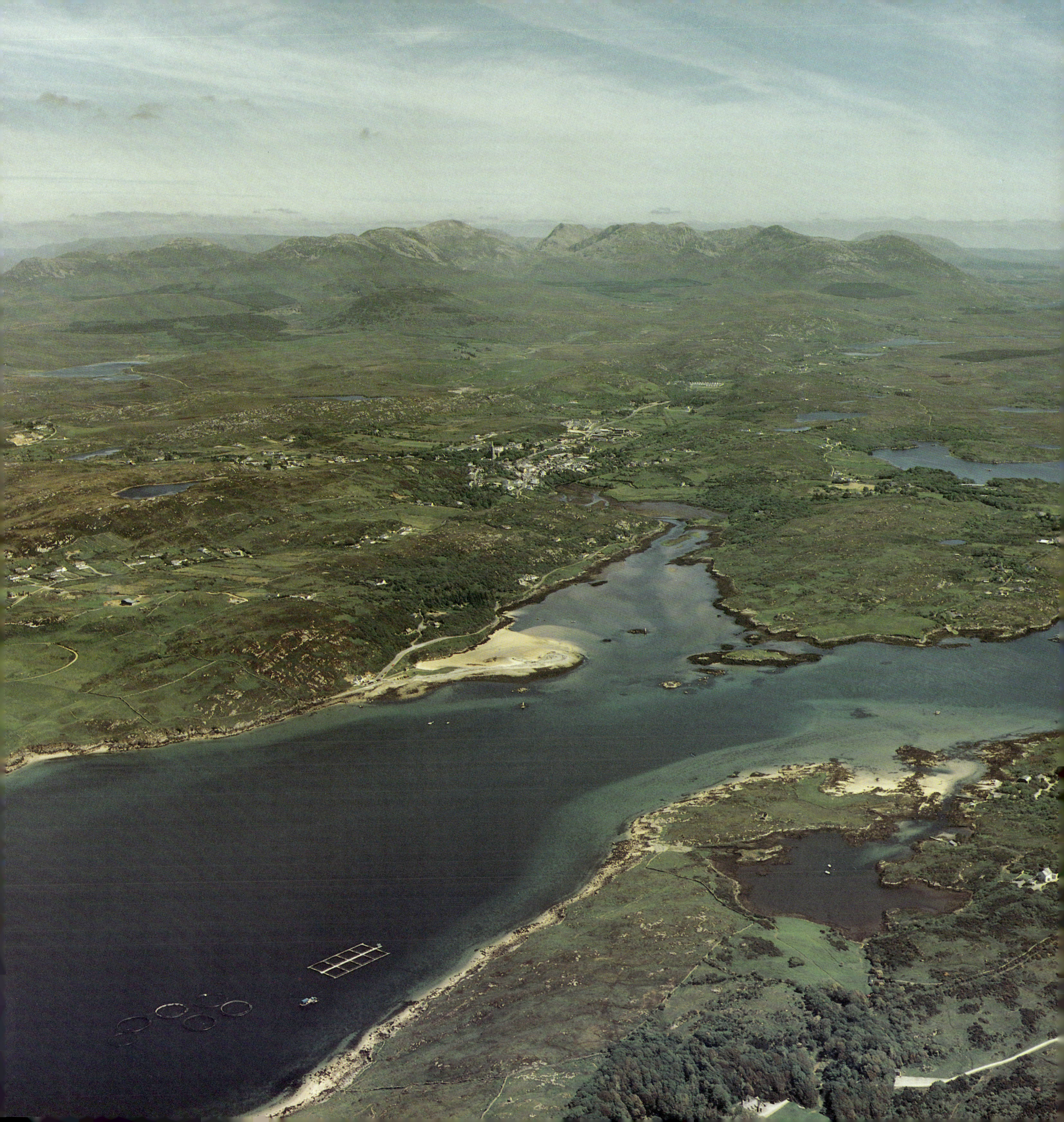

The harbour and pier on the island of Inishbofin, with Inishturk just to the north.
Right, Ireland's only fjord Killary, heading deep into Connemara.

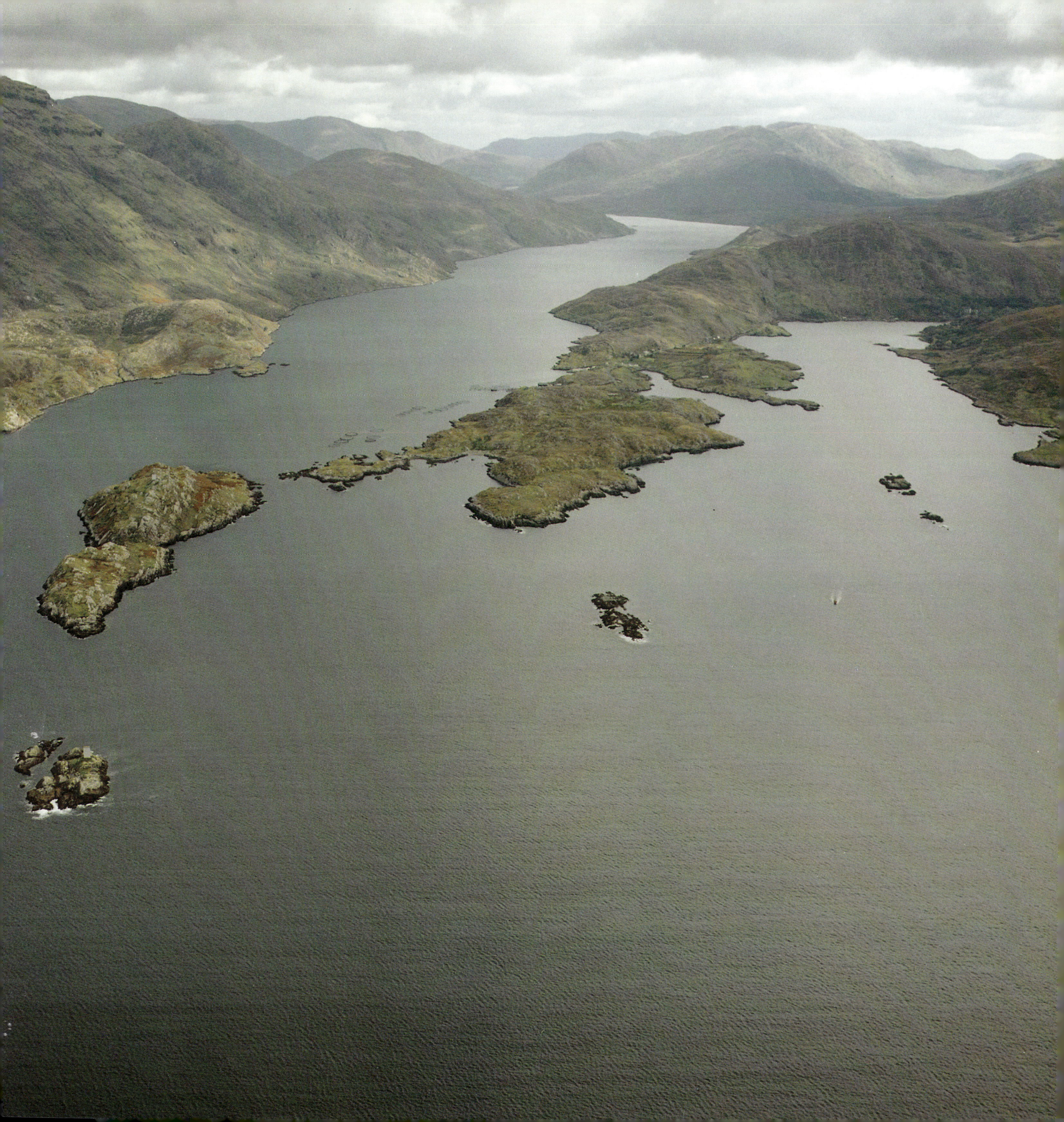

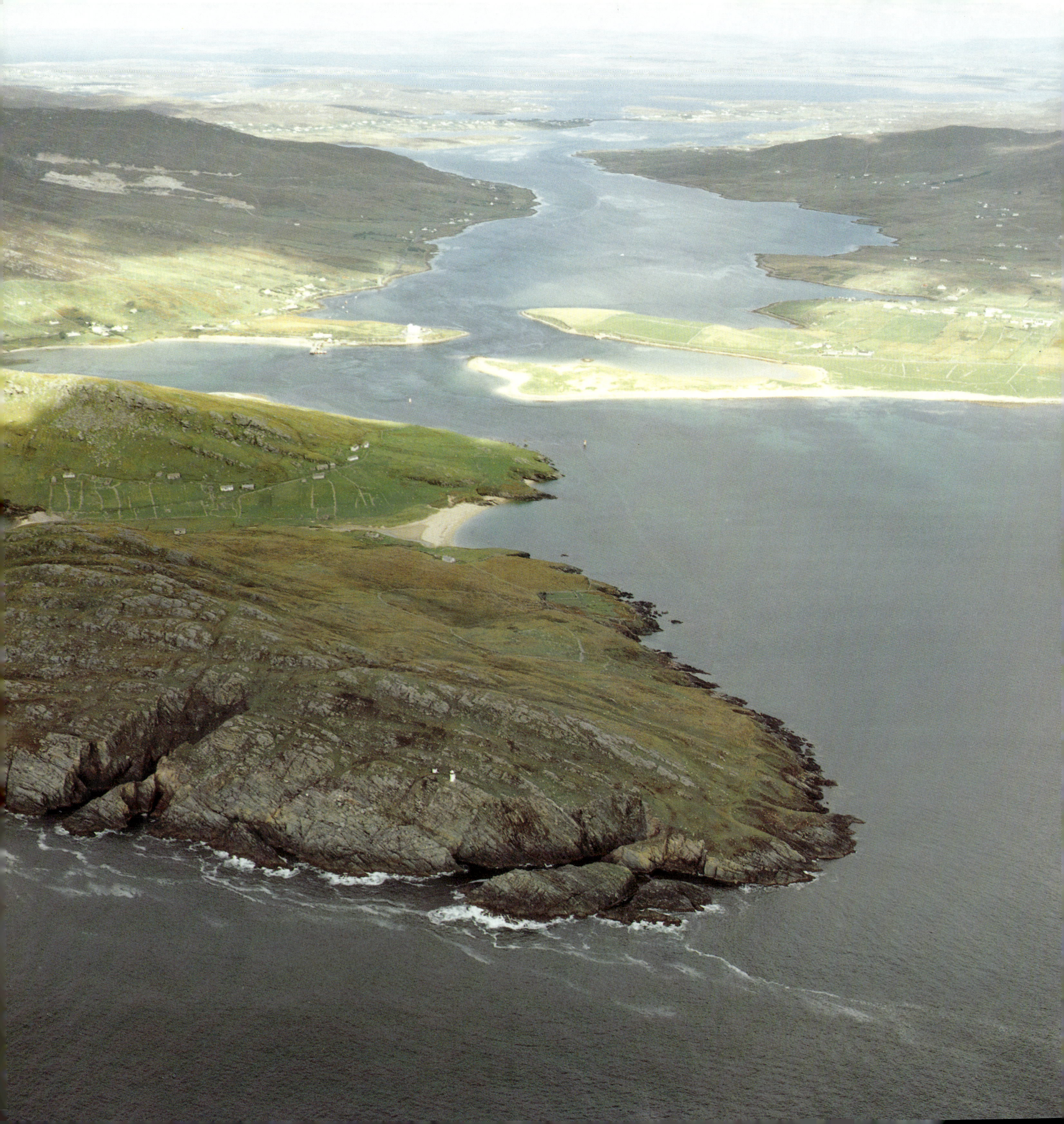

The southern part of Achill Sound and above,
the bridge from Achill to the island of Ireland.

Moyran Point on the Mullet peninsula and right,
Frenchport with Eagle Island and lighthouse in the distance.

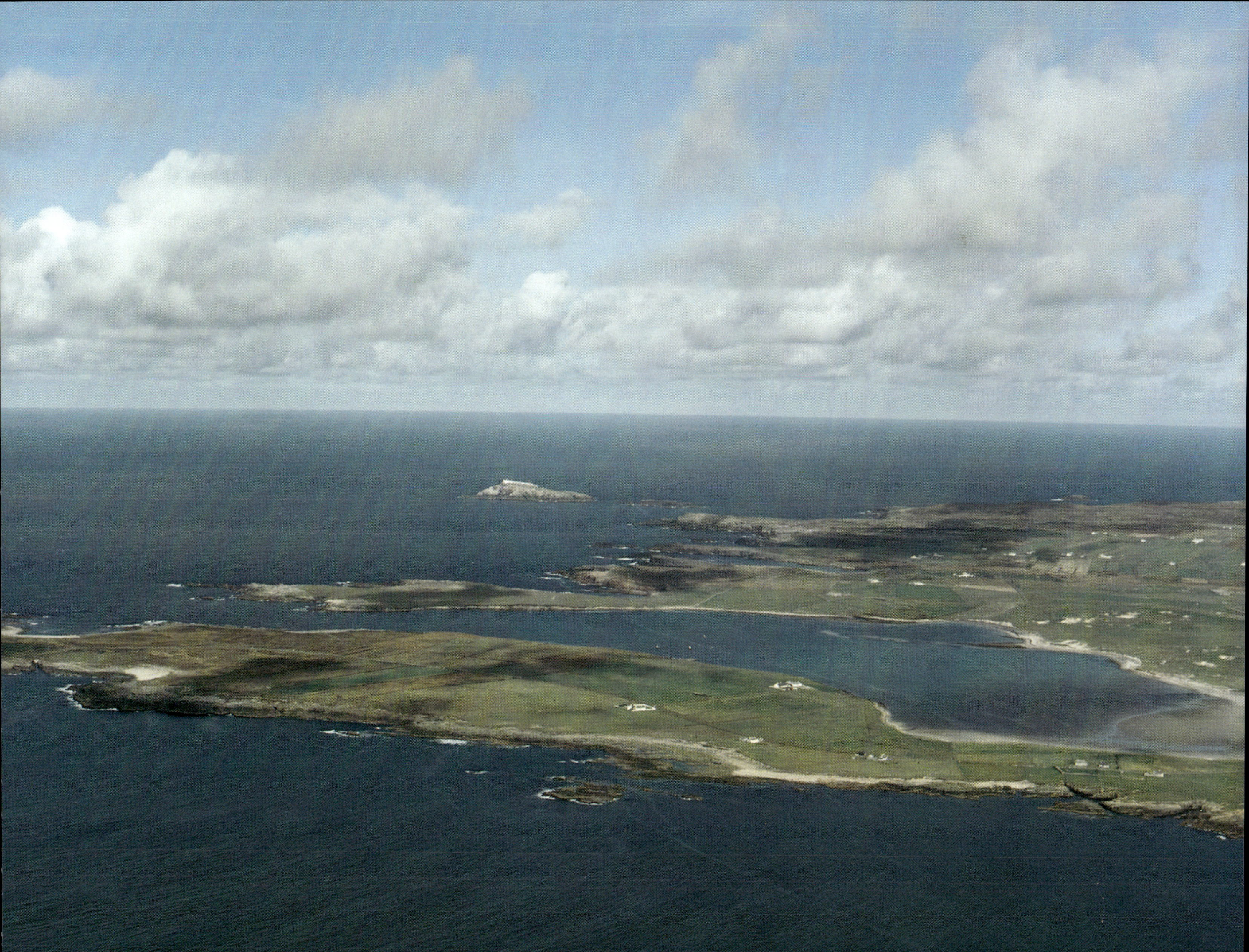

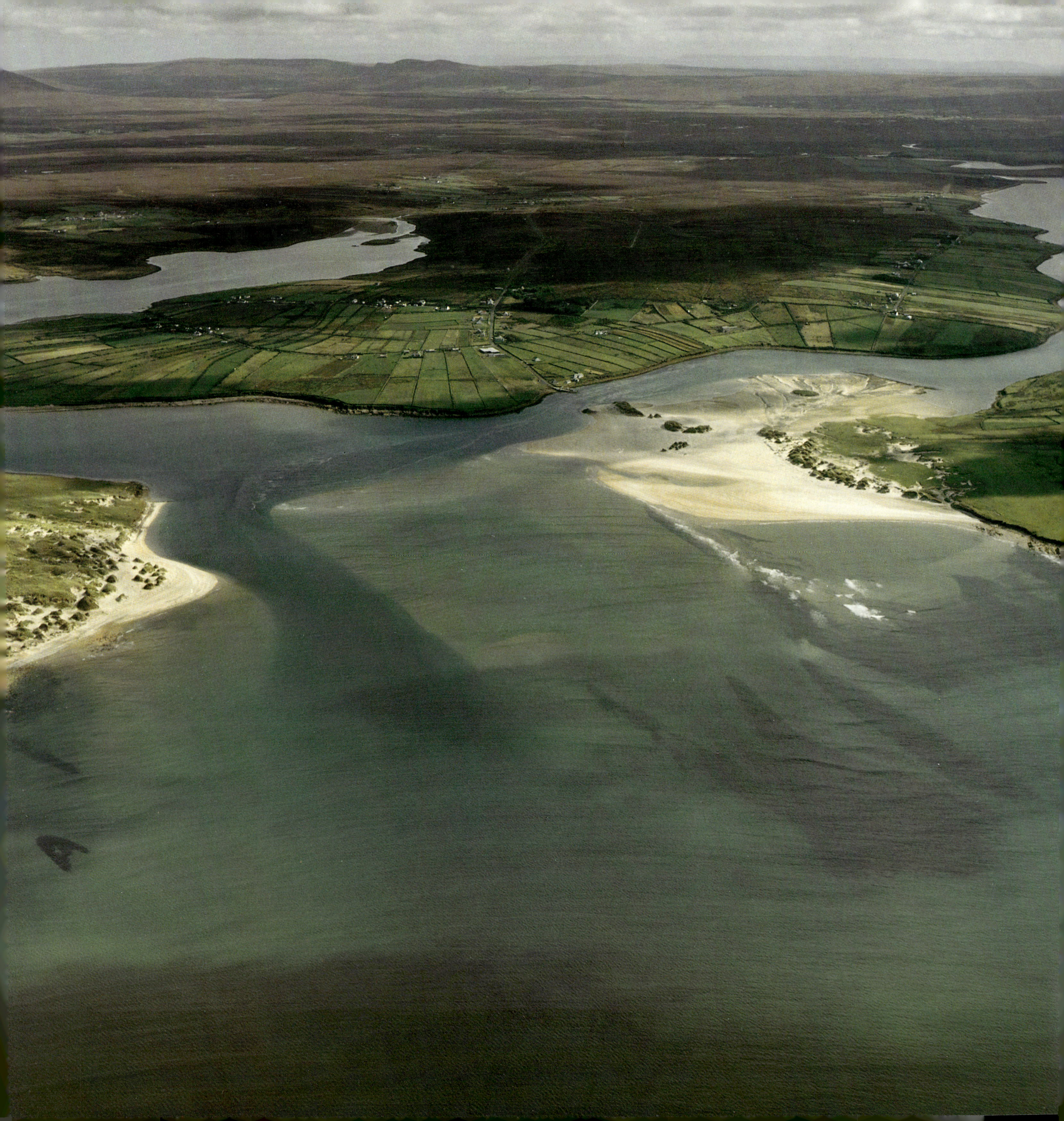

The sandy channel into the anchorage of Rossport
and above, Killala in North Mayo.

Coney Island leading to Rosses Point near Sligo
with Ben Bulben rising away in the distance.

The final part of our flight takes us around the coastline of Ulster and over the top of Ireland.

We begin by flying past Killybegs and Teelin on the southern coast of County Donegal and then head north past Burtonport and Bloody Foreland before flying out over Tory, the most northerly inhabited island around our coastline.

We now sweep over Sheephaven with its many sandy beaches, and head down Mulroy Bay and up Lough Swilly to reach Trawbreega Bay near Malin Head and the end of our flight over Donegal.

We continue our journey by flying east over Portstewart in County Derry, Portrush and Port Ballintrae on the north Antrim coast before heading out to Rathlin Island, the north-east corner of Ireland.

We now fly south over Larne on the Antrim coast and finally Carrickfergus overlooking Belfast Lough. Getting closer to the end of our journey, we fly over Bangor in County Down and Donaghadee. We curve around Strangford Lough and fly south over Ardglass, Annalong and Kilkeel, all on the south shore of County Down, bringing us to the end of our flight around IRELAND, *Our Island Home.*

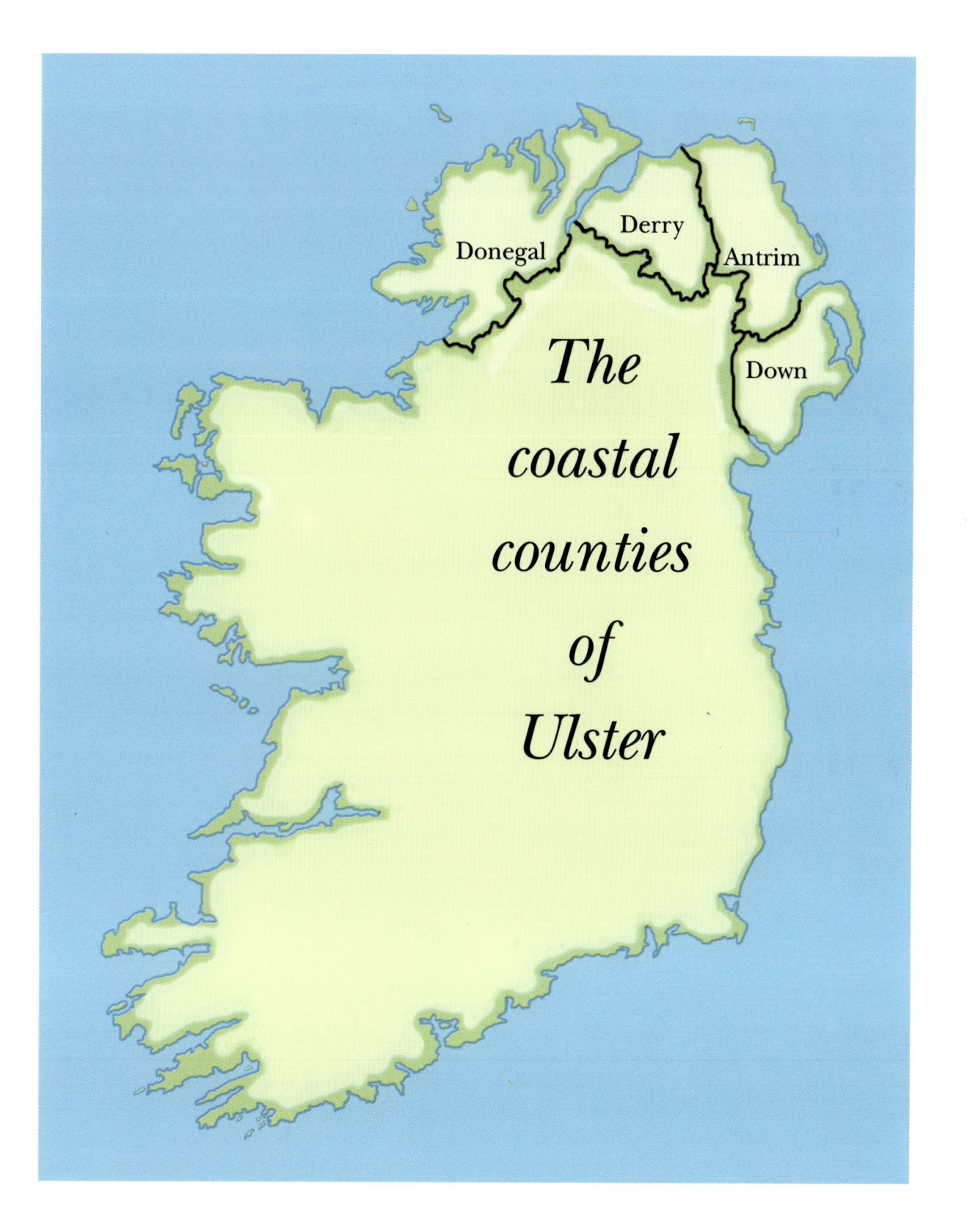

The coastal counties of Ulster

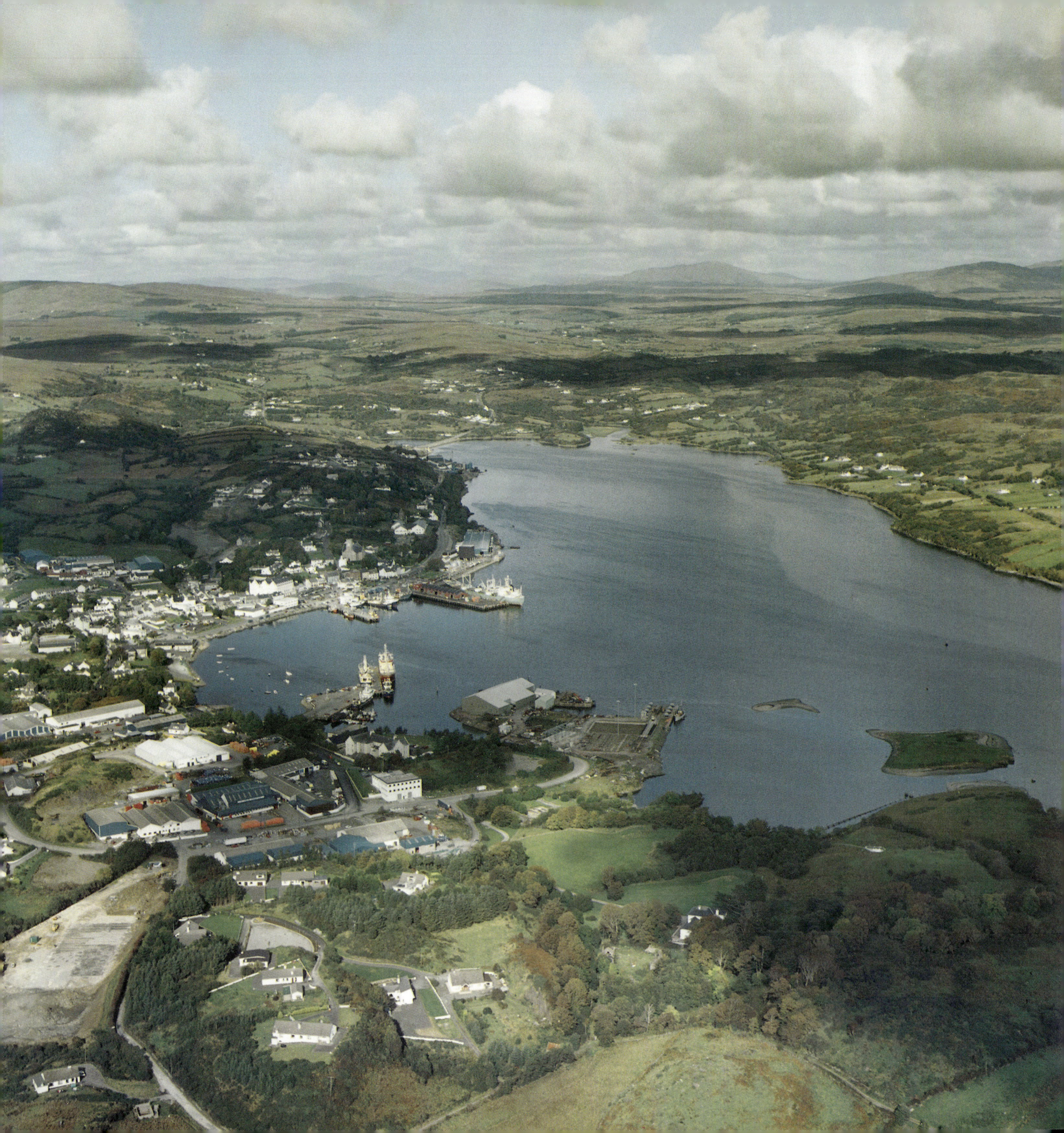

The important fishing port of Killybegs in County Donegal.
Above, Teelin, a sheltered bay on the south Donegal coast.

Above, Burtonport, overlooking Aran Sound and right,
the Island of Gola stretching across the picture with Bloody Foreland
on the top right hand corner and Tory Island in the distance.

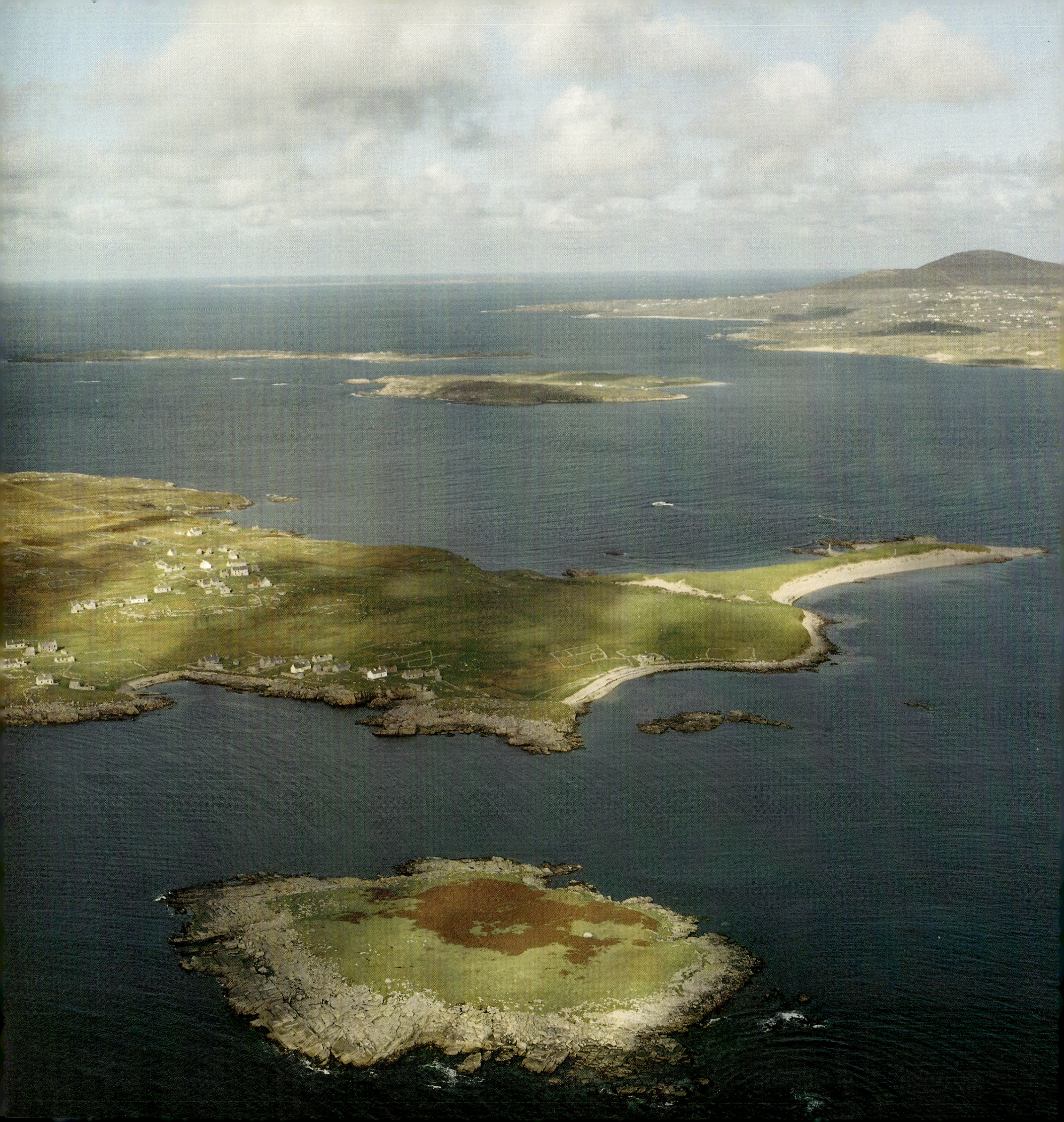

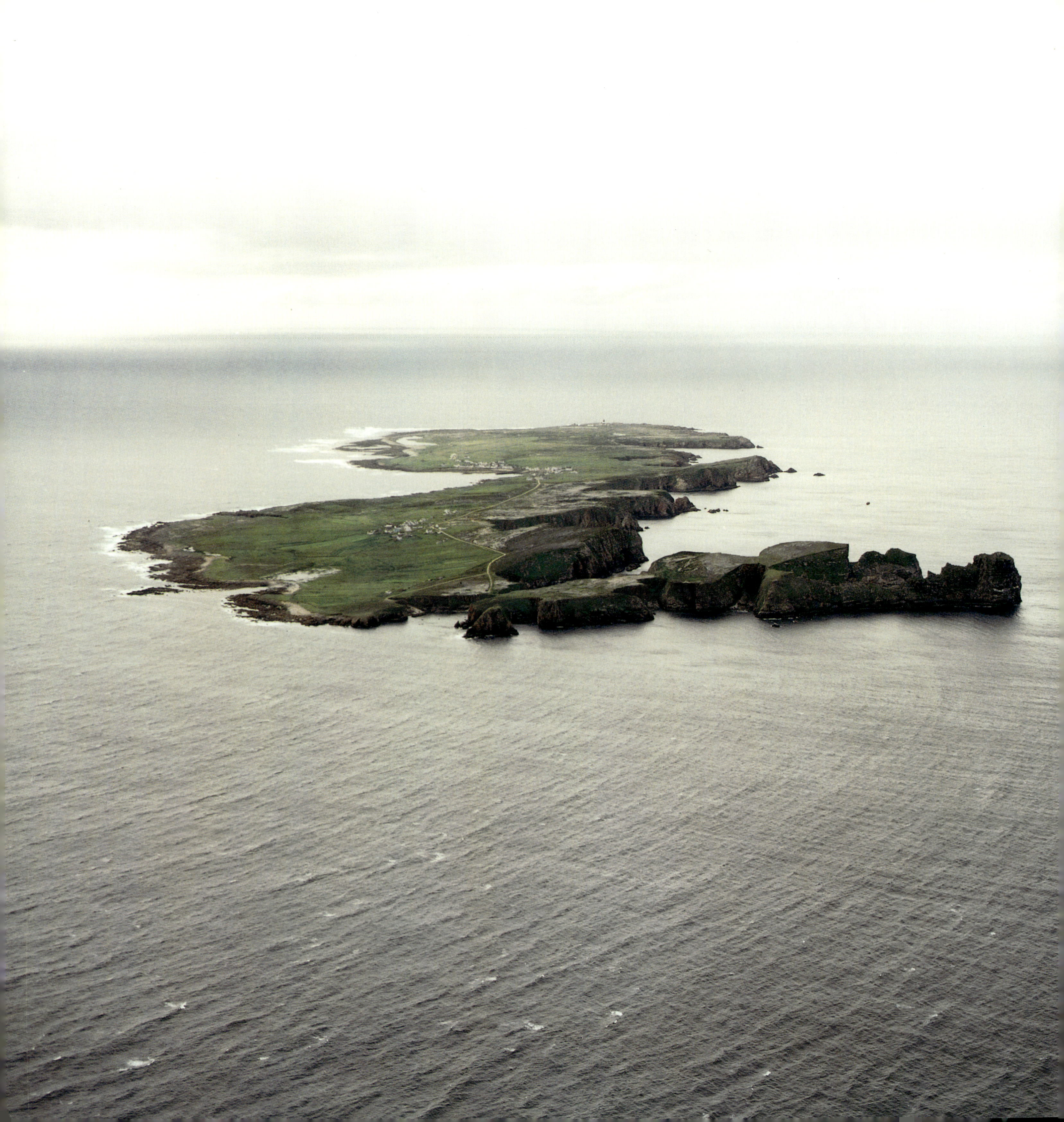

Tory Island, off the north-west corner of Ireland on the left, and above, the two settlements of West Town and East Town.

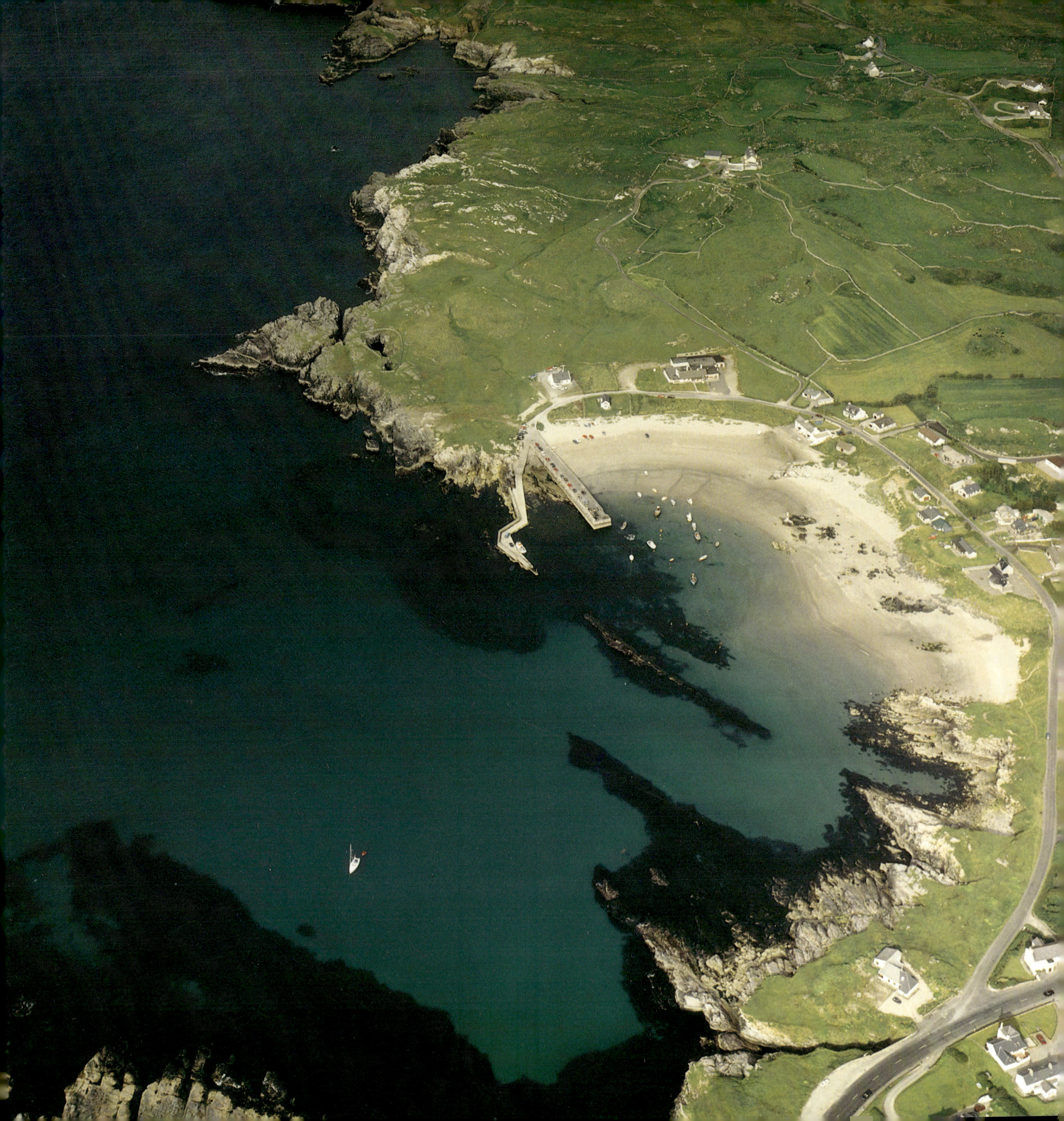

Portnablahy on the southern side of Dunfanaghy Bay in Sheephaven, north Donegal and right, Marble Hill Strand, a little bit to the east.

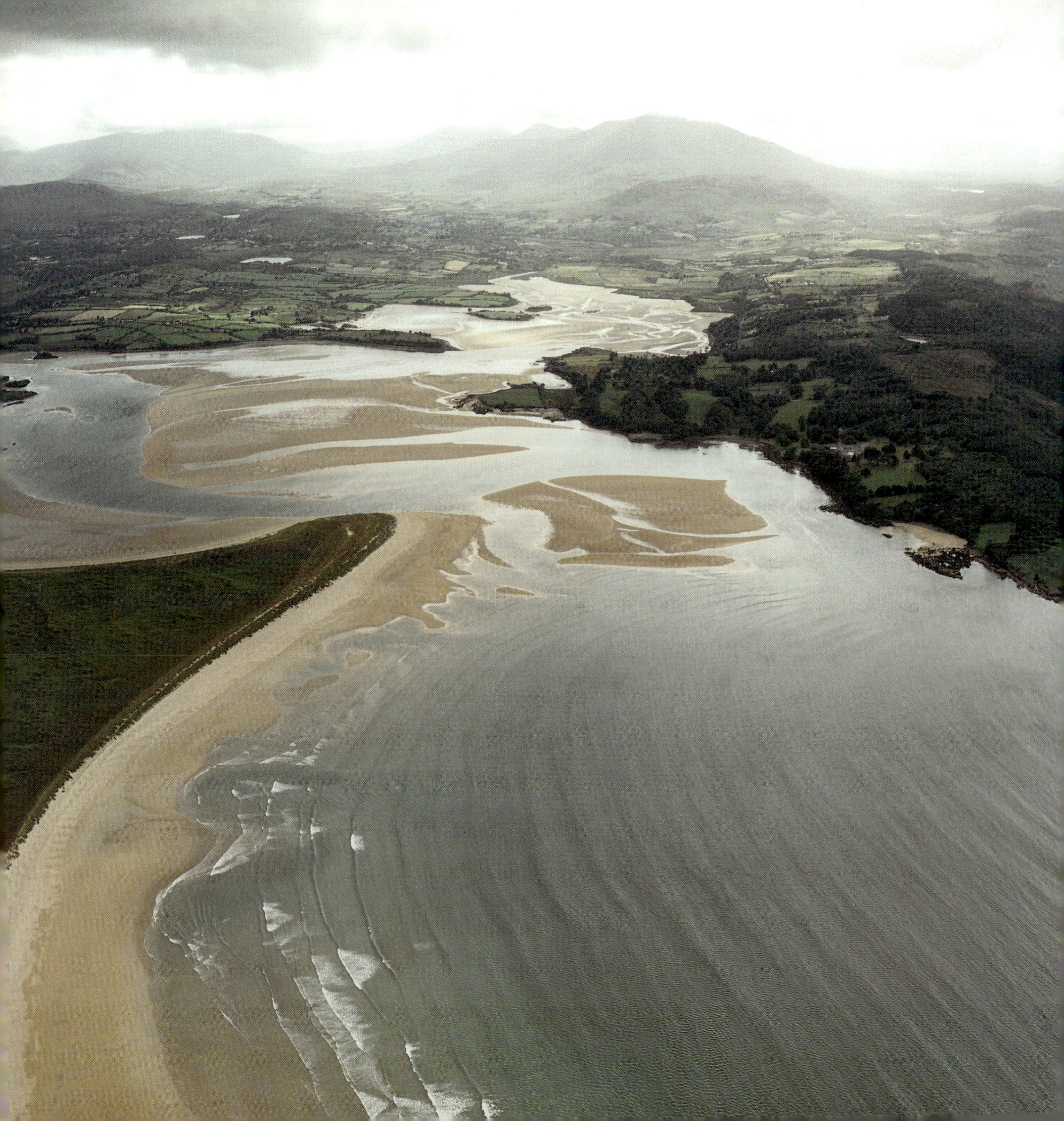

At the eastern end of Sheephaven is the sandy estuary at Ards Bay and above, the large and popular beach at Downings.

Mulroy Bay, leading deep into north Donegal and right, Milford Port and Quay at the southern end of Mulroy and looking towards Broadwater.

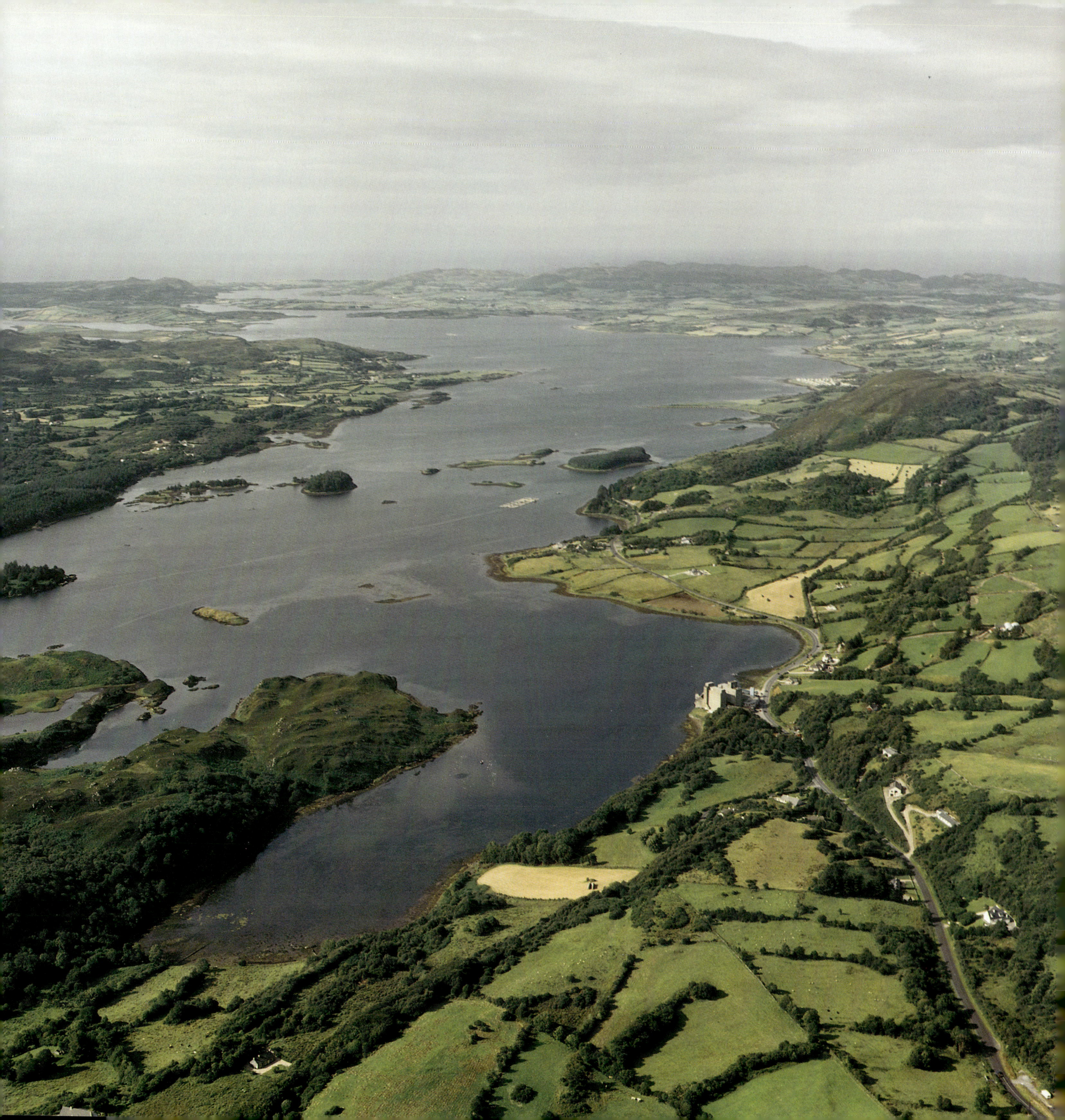

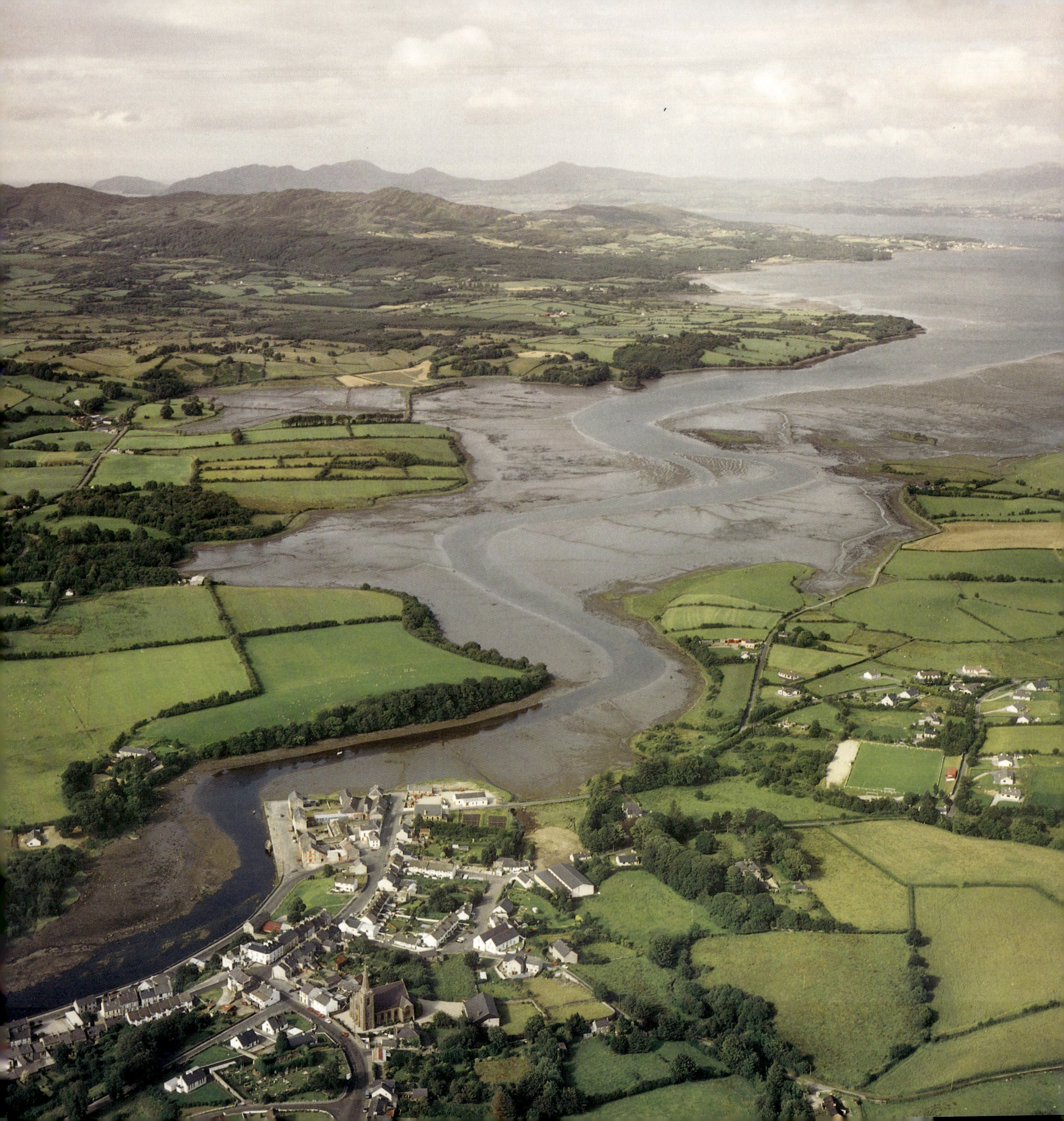

Low tide showing the channel towards Rathmelton and above,
Rathmullen on the western shore of Lough Swilley
as it stretches 25 miles (40 km) into Donegal.

The Martello Tower and beaches at Macamish on Lough Swilley and right, Trawbreega Bay just to the south of Malin Head, the most northerly tip of *Our Island Home*.

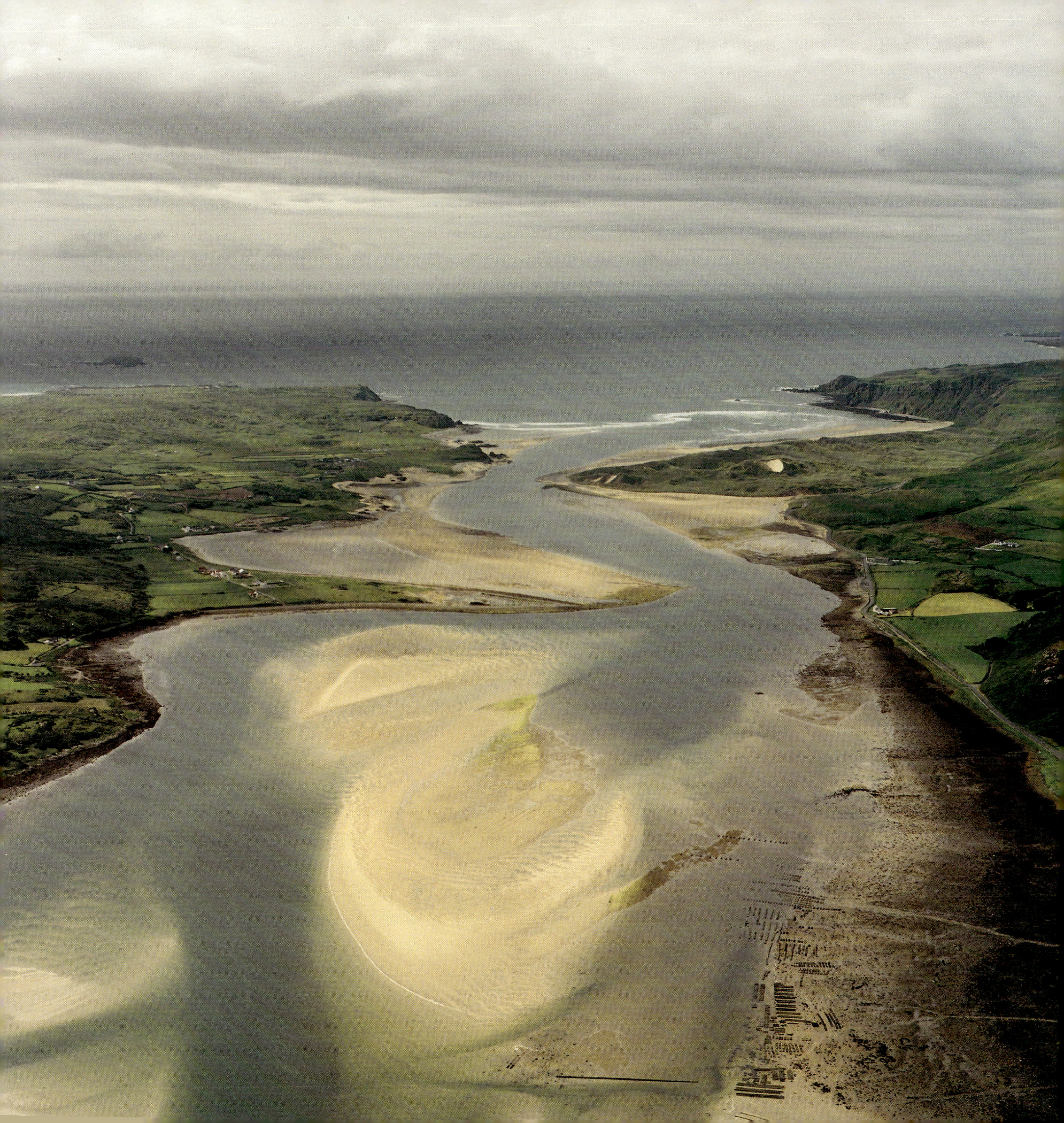

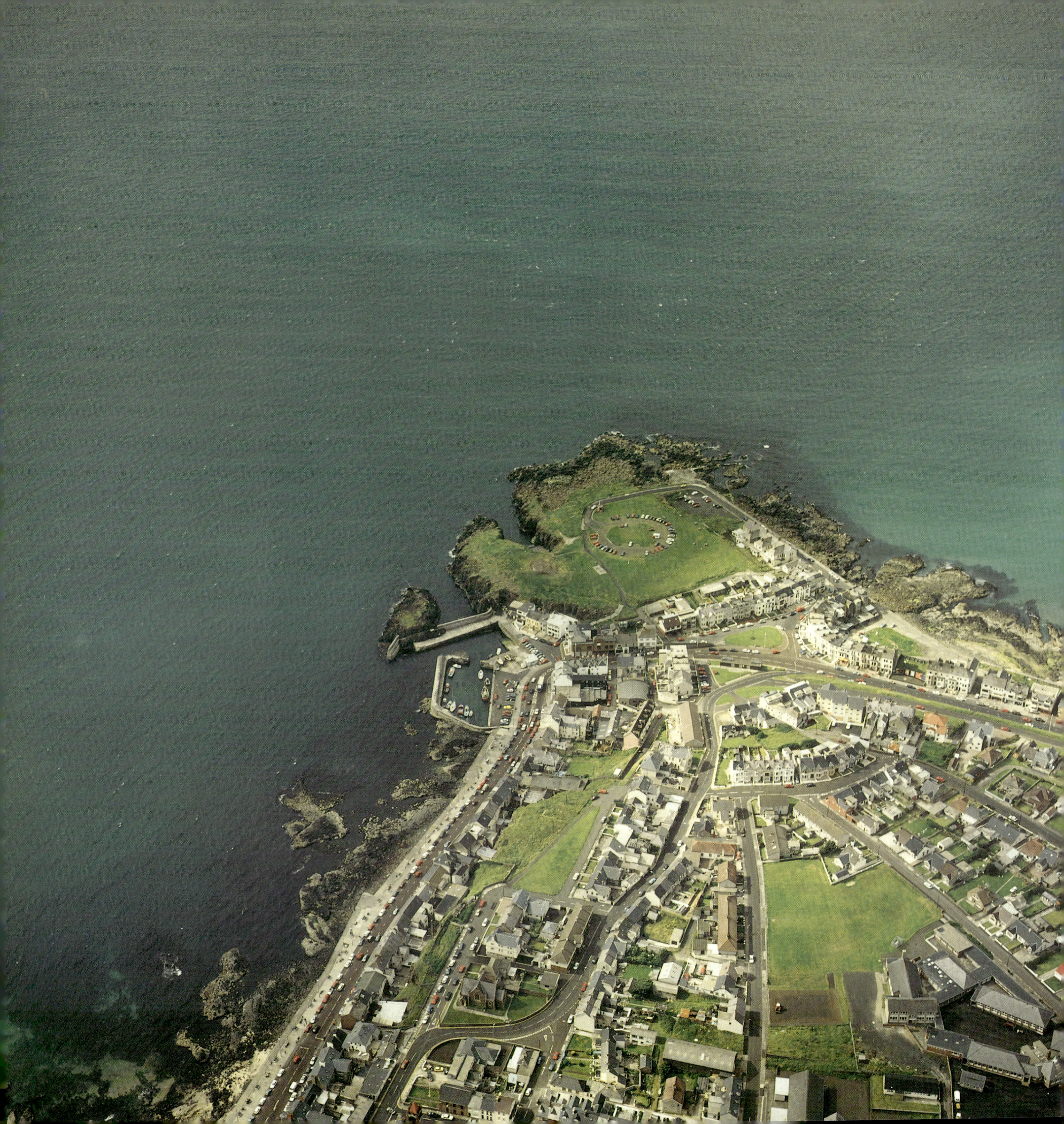

The town of Portstewart in County Derry
and above, Portrush, on the north coast of Antrim.

The bay at Portballintrae and right,
Church Bay, Rathlin Island, the north-east corner of Ireland.

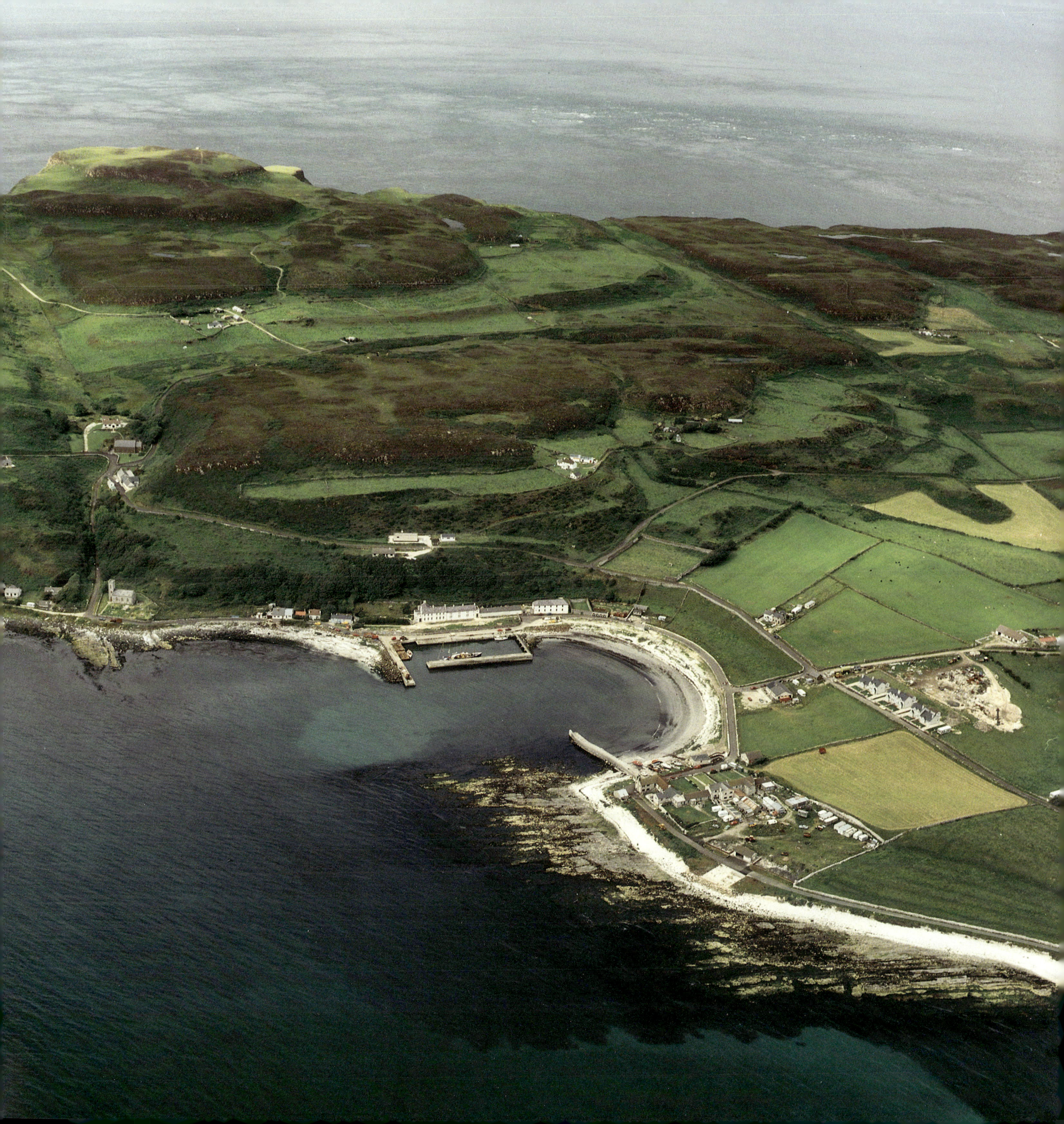

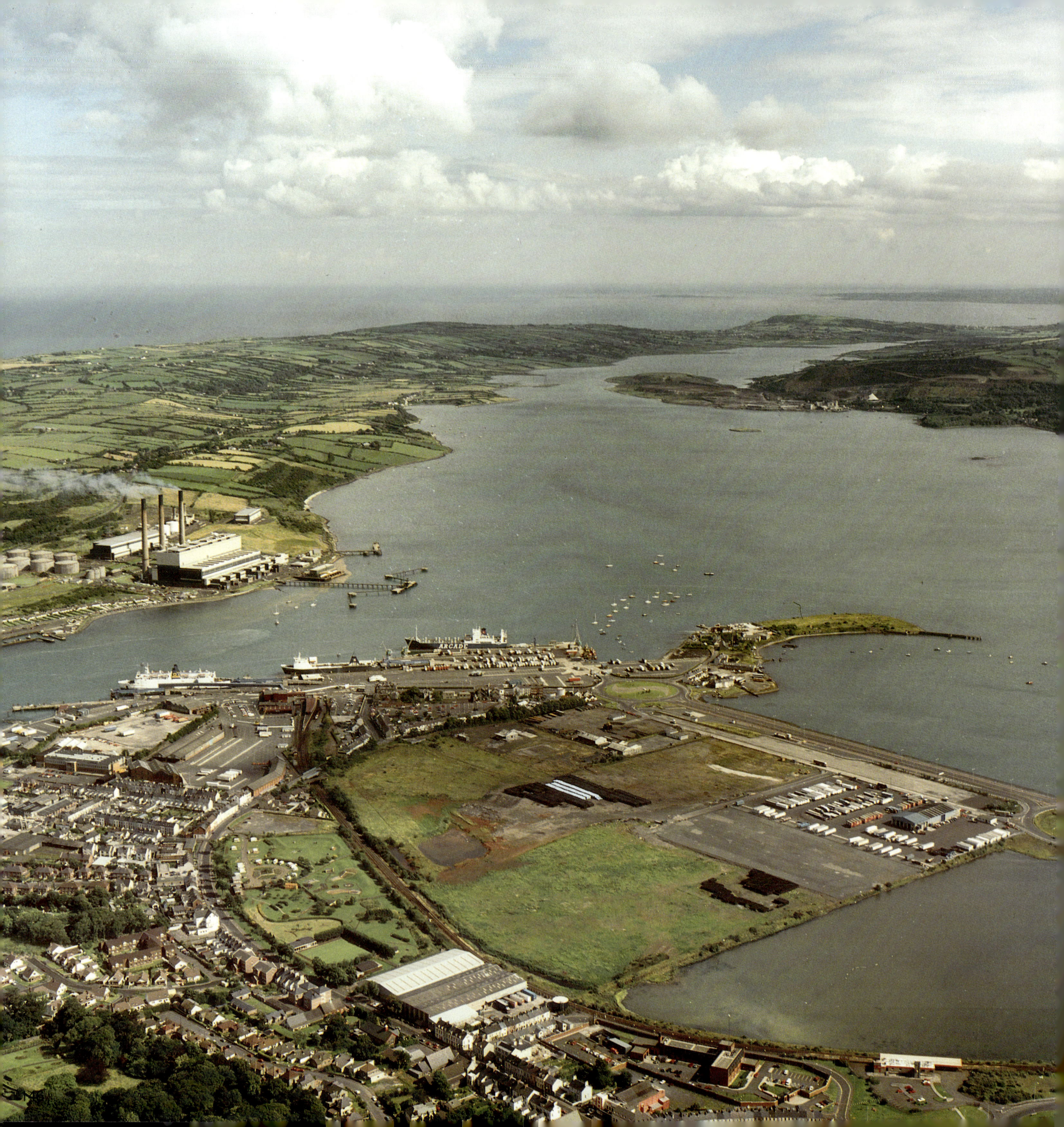

Larne Lough in Antrim, looking south and with the entrance to Belfast Lough in the distance.
Above, the ferryport of Larne looking towards Scotland
with the Mull of Kintyre in the distance and Arran Island in the Clyde top right.

Carrickfergus on the southern shore of Antrim and overlooking Belfast Lough.
Right, the town, harbour and marina of Bangor in County Down,
with Belfast Lough heading west to the City of Belfast.

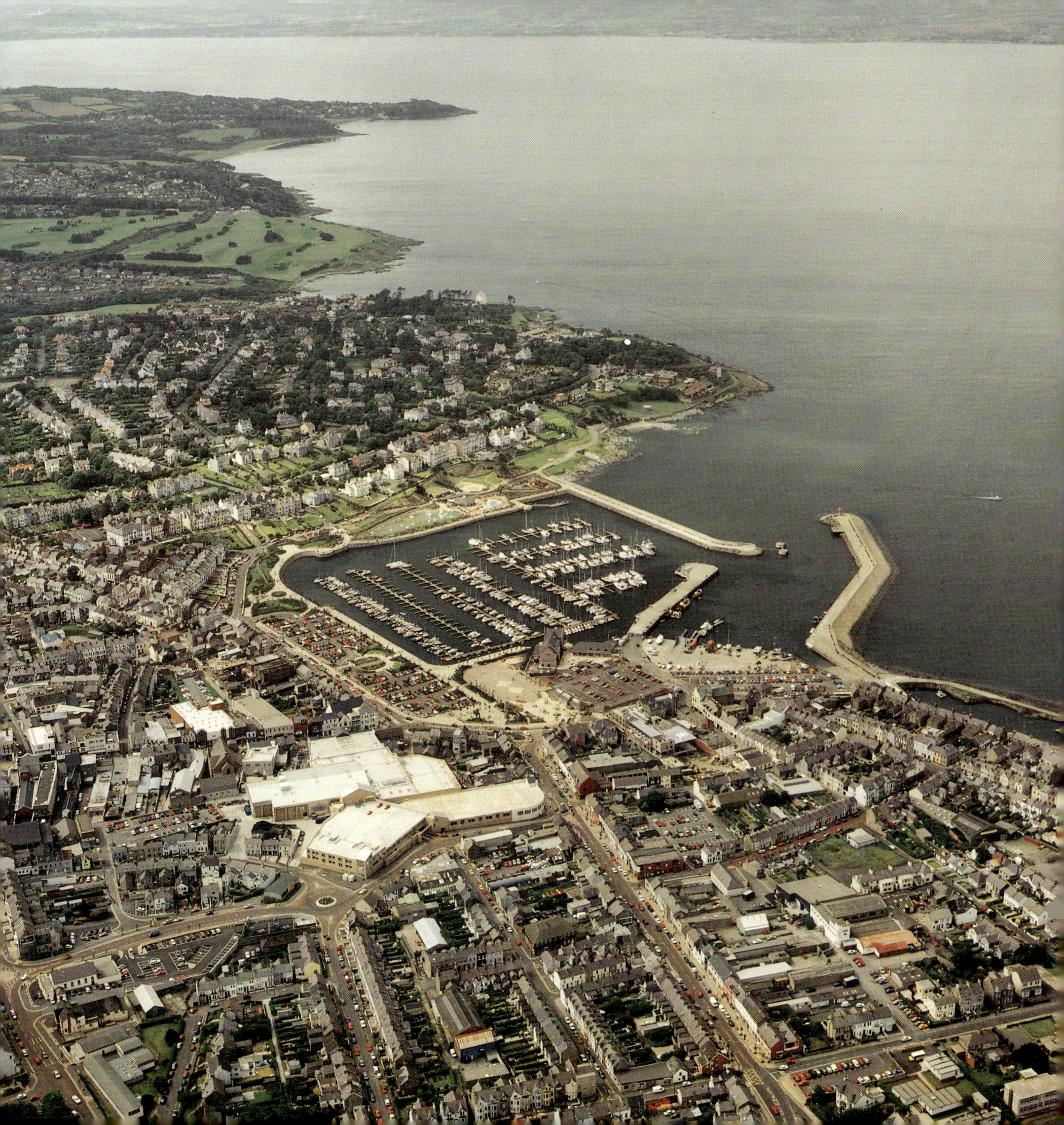

Donaghadee and Copeland Sound on the shore of the Ards peninsula
and right, yachts moored at Whiterock just to the south
of Sketrick Island in Strangford Lough.

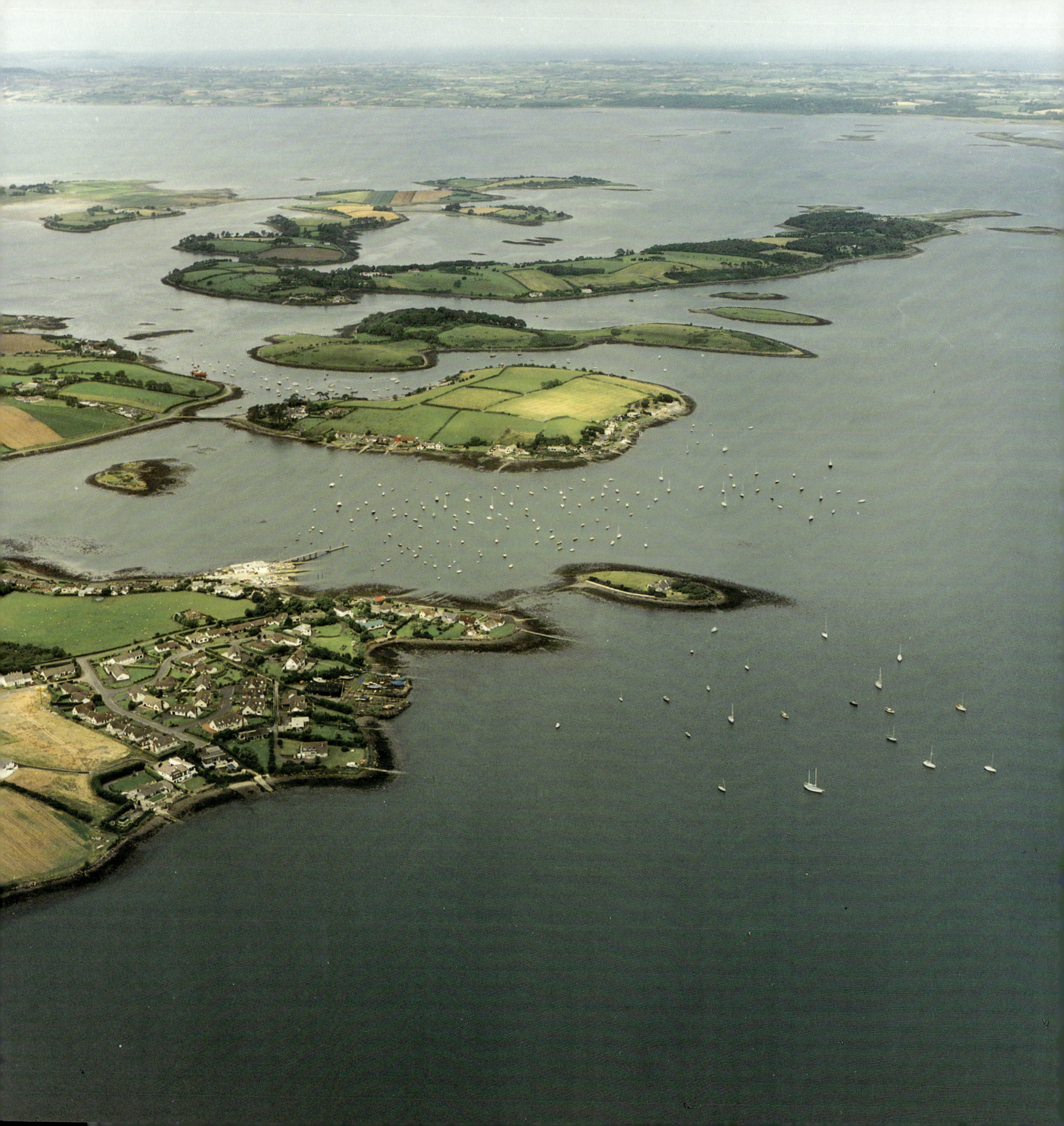

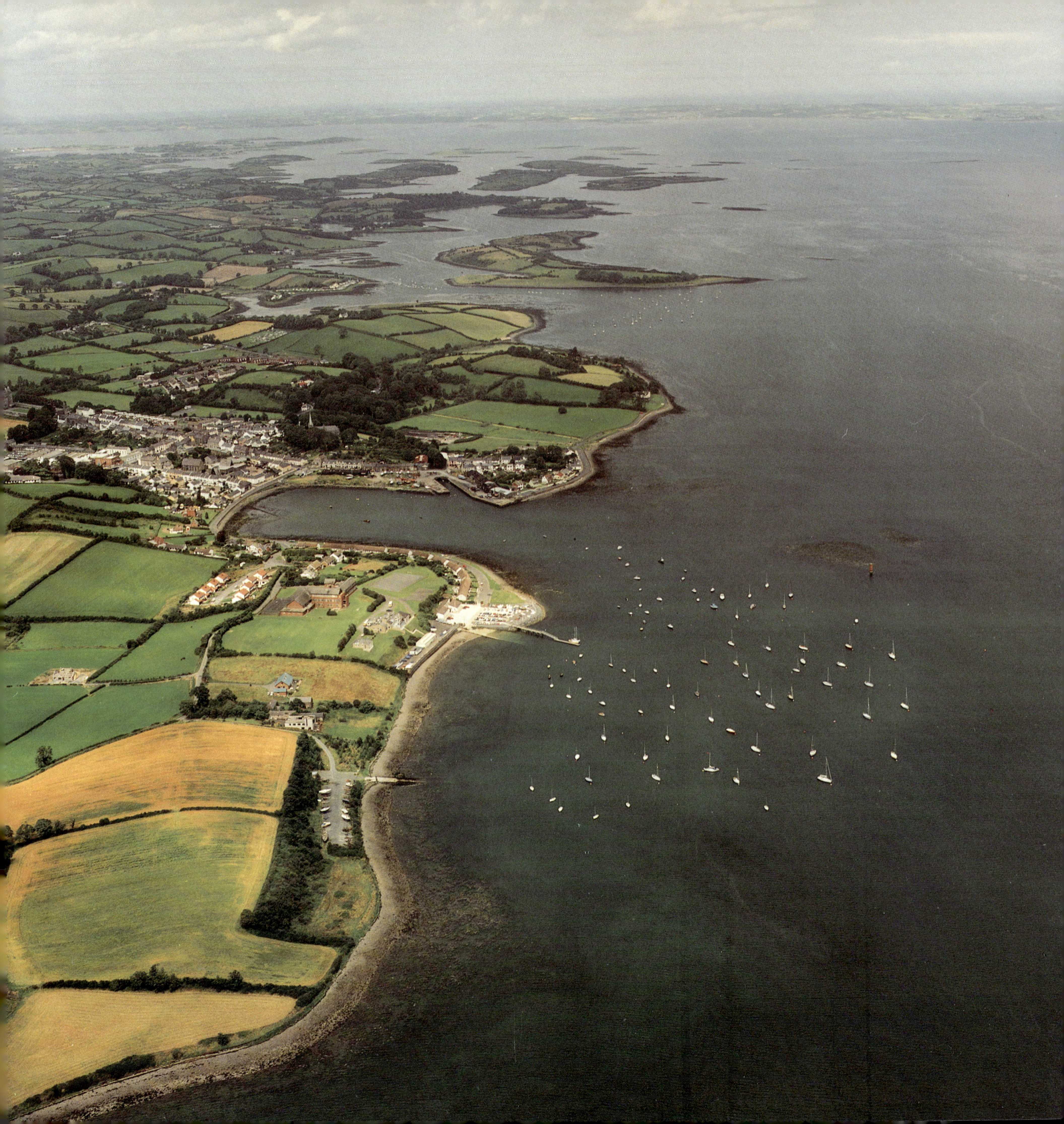

Killyleagh with the western shoreline of Strangford Lough heading north towards Newtownards and above, Quoile in County Down at the southern end of Strangford Lough – more sheep than yachts !

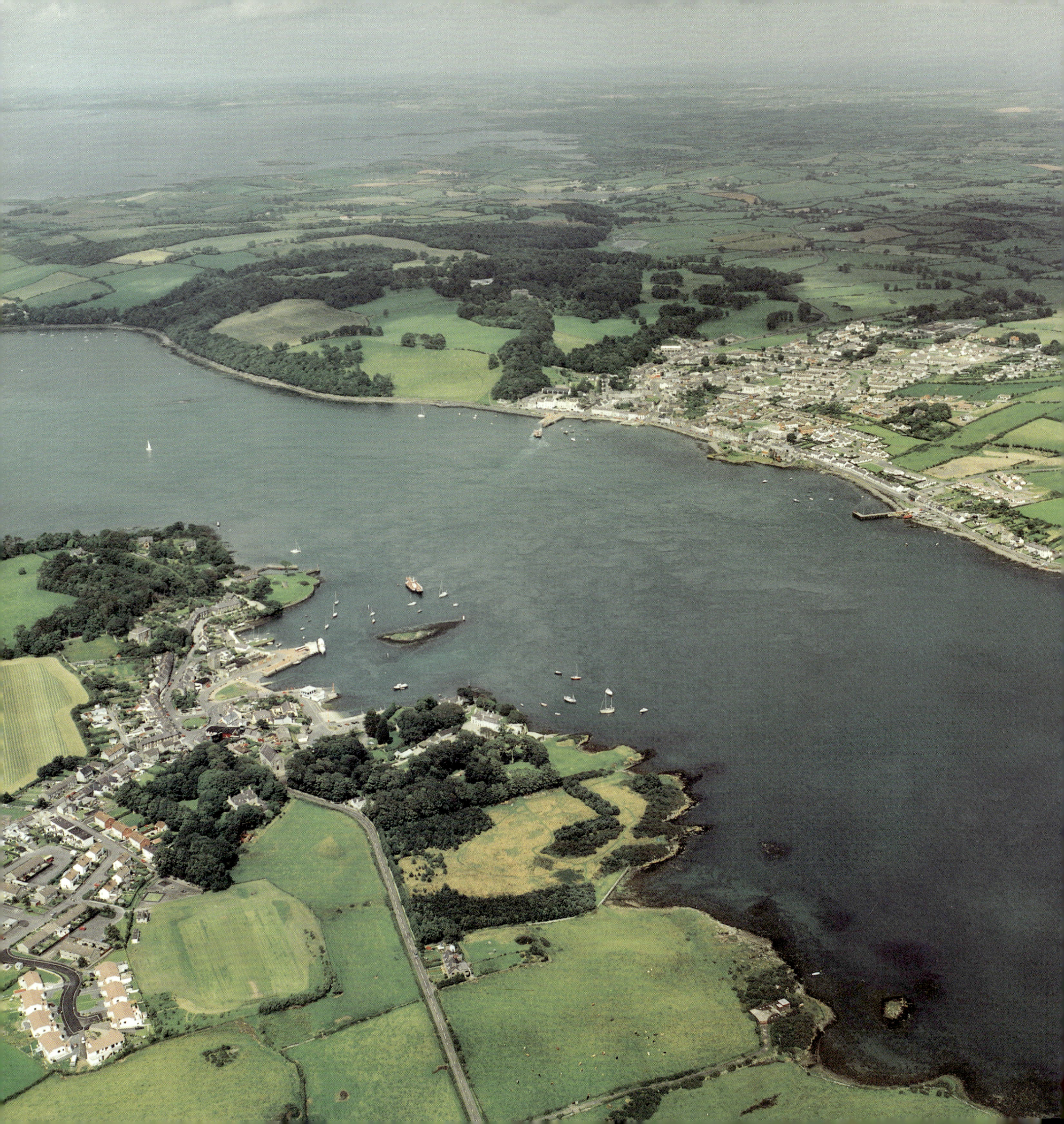

Strangford on the left looking towards Portaferry at the base of the Ards peninsula
and above, Strangford Narrows leading into the Lough.

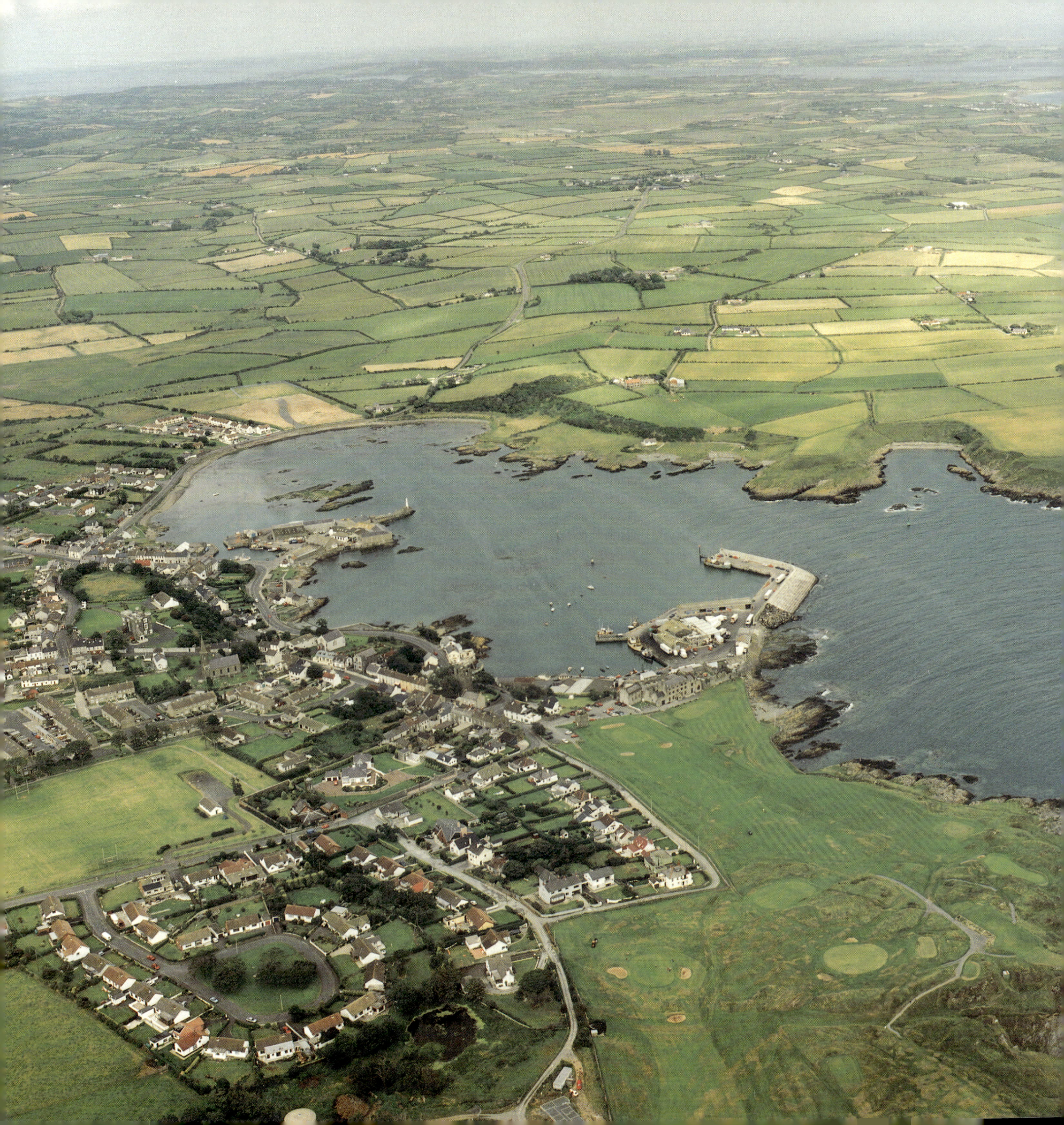

The pier and harbour of Ardglass and above,
the wee harbour at Annalong, both in County Down.

The important fishing port of Kilkeel in County Down, close to Carlingford Lough and the start of the book !

INDEX

Achill Bridge	119
Achill Sound	118
Annalong	157
Aran Islands	106
Aran Sound/Burtonport	128
Ardglass	156
Ardmore	40
Ards Bay	134
Arklow	28
Asgard II	29
Ballycotton	43
Ballyhack/Passage East	34
Ballyvaughan	98
Baltimore	60
Bangor and Belfast Lough	149
Bantry House & Yachts	70
Bantry Town	69
Bantry/Whiddy/Glengarriff	71
Blarney Castle	51
Blasket Island	90
Boyne River	12
Bullock Harbour/Sandycove	24
Cahersiveen	85
Cape Clear 'North Harbour'	61
Carlingford Lough	11
Carrickfergus	148
Carrigaholt	95
Castletown Berehaven	74
Castletownshend	59
Clifden & 12 Bens	115
Clifden Bay	114
Cobh Crescent	45
Cobh QE2	46
Cork from East	48
Cork from West	50
Cork Shandon	49
Courtown	30
Crookhaven	66
Crosshaven	52
Dalkey	25
Deenish Island	80
Derrynane	81
Dingle Harbour	88
Dingle Town & mountains	89
Donaghadee	150
Dooks	86
Downings	135
Dublin Castle	21
Dublin Merrion Sq	20
Dublin Phoenix Park	18
Dublin Port	17
Dublin Portobello	19
Dublin Trinity/O'Connell St.	22
Dun Laoghaire	23
Dunboy	74
Duncannon	33
Dunfanaghy Bay	132
Dungarvan	39
Dunmanus Bay	68
Dunmore East	37
Dursey Island Bull/Cow/Calf	76
East Ferry	44
Fastnet	67
Fenit	91
Frenchport	121
Galway	102
Galway	103
Garinish Island	73
Glengarriff	72
Glounthaune	47
Gola Is. Bloodyforeland	129
Greystones	26
Horse & Castle Islands	64
Howth	16
Inch	87
Inchydoney	57
Inishbofin/Inishturk	116
Inishmann	107
Inishmore/Dun Aengus	109
Inishmore/Kilronan	108
Kenmare Bay & Town	78
Kilkee	96
Kilkeel	158
Kilkieran Bay	110
Kilkieran Cove	111
Killala	123
Killaloe	93
Killary	117
Killmakilloge	77
Killmore Quay	32
Killybegs	126
Killyleagh	152
Kilrush	94
Kinsale Charles Fort	56
Kinsale from North—West	55
Kinsale from South—East	54
Kinsale Town	53
Kinvara	100
Larne Lough	146
Larne/Mull of Kintyre	147
Limerick	92
Long Island Sound	65
Macamish Anchorage	140
Malahide	15
Marblehill Bay	133
Milford	137
Moher — cliffs of	97
Mullett Penninsula	120
Mulroy Bay	136
Naval Review	45
New Grange	13
New Harbour (Rinville)	101
Piper Sound	75
Portballintrae	144
Portrush	143
Portstewart	142
Quoile	153
Rathlin Island Church Bay	145
Rathmelton	138
Rathmullen	139
Reenard/Knightstown	84
Rossaveal	105
Rosses Point	124
Rosslare	31
Rossport	122
Roundstone	112
Roundstone Beach	113
Schull	62
Schull Yachts	63
Skelligs — Beehive Huts	83
Skelligs — Steps	82
Skerries	14
Sneem River	79
Spiddal	104
Strangford Narrows	155
Strangford/Portaferry	154
Teelin	127
Tory Island	130
Tory Island	131
Tramore	38
Trawbreega Bay	141
Union Hall/Glandore	58
Waterford	36
Whiterock	151
Wicklow	27
Youghal	42